Tragedy on Jackass Mountain

ALSO BY CHARLES SCHEIDEMAN
Policing the Fringe: The Curious Life of a Small-Town Mountie

TRAGEDY ON JACKASS MOUNTAIN

MORE STORIES FROM A SMALL-TOWN MOUNTIE

Charles Scheideman

HARBOUR PUBLISHING

Copyright © 2011 Charles Scheideman
1 2 3 4 5 — 15 14 13 12 11

All rights reserved. No part of this publication may be reproduced, stored in a retrieval system or transmitted, in any form or by any means, without prior permission of the publisher or, in the case of photocopying or other reprographic copying, a licence from Access Copyright, www.accesscopyright.ca, 1-800-893-5777, info@accesscopyright.ca.

Harbour Publishing Co. Ltd.
P.O. Box 219, Madeira Park, BC, V0N 2H0
www.harbourpublishing.com

Author's note: While the stories in this book are all true, some names and details have been changed in order to protect the privacy of individuals.
Cover photograph of the highway view from Jackass Mountain by Doug Lavoie
Shell Map of British Columbia, Alberta, Saskatchewan and Manitoba, 1956, courtesy David Rumsey Historical Map Collection
All other photographs from the author's collection
Edited by Betty Keller
Cover design by Teresa Karbashewski
Text design by Mary White
Printed on FSC certified stock using soy-based ink
Printed and bound in Canada
Harbour Publishing acknowledges financial support from the Government of Canada through the Canada Book Fund and the Canada Council for the Arts, and from the Province of British Columbia through the BC Arts Council and the Book Publishing Tax Credit.

 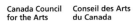 

Library and Archives Canada Cataloguing in Publication

Scheideman, Charles
   Tragedy on Jackass Mountain : more stories from a small-town Mountie / Charles Scheideman.

ISBN 978-1-55017-550-9

   1. Scheideman, Charles. 2. Royal Canadian Mounted Police—Biography.
3. Royal Canadian Mounted Police—Anecdotes. 4. British
Columbia—Biography.
I. Title.

HV7911.S343A3 2011   363.2092   C2011-900564-6

To
my wife Patricia,
our children Howard, Sherry and Christopher,
all those with whom I worked
&
RCMP Reg. #23794 Peter David Eakins 1965–2000
and RCMP Reg. #25162 Daryl Wayne Bakewell
1966–1975 & 1978–1987.
May they rest in peace.
"Without Fear, Favour or Affection"

Contents

Introduction	9
The Origins of a Mountie	11
The Canada Goose	17
Police Training	36
A Training Experience	41
My First Posting	47
Jock Straps	53
Salmo's Flying Ace	65
Born for a Bad End	71
Death in the Bush	76
The One That Almost Got Away	81
Reality Lost	86
Pinky and the Bad Guys	89
Giants at Alcohol Lake	96
Corporal Punishment	101
Jackass Mountain—A Hard Climb	114
Bad Luck on Jackass Mountain	122

The Second Man	*128*
Transport versus Greyhound	*134*
Cold Little Feet	*142*
Kids and Trains	*145*
A Native Rancher	*149*
A Professional Thief	*156*
A Missing Aircraft	*162*
Golden Flying Deer	*167*
Bugaboo Helicopter Skiing	*172*
The Runaway Train	*178*
A Well-Oiled Trucker	*185*
Struck From Above	*190*
A Really Cool Driver	*194*
A Tough Choice	*198*
Quesnel's Missing Man	*205*
The Lead-Lined Camera Case	*210*
Big Coal Mines and Big Money	*213*
The Fighting Fools	*217*

Constable Charles Scheideman, 1968

Introduction

There are a number of books and stories out in the world that detail the glories of the Royal Canadian Mounted Police and one cannot help but hear the strains of "Rose Marie" as one reads them. Such stories have their place in history but not in my writing.

My service with the RCMP was a positive experience for the most part, and although some of my anecdotes may suggest that I was in constant disagreement with the organization, this was not the case. It just happens that it's the tales with a little conflict and disagreement that provide the most interesting reading. The majority of happenings in my long career with the RCMP were carried out smoothly and efficiently, and I had the pleasure of working with a few truly great men and with a large number of above average people.

The Origins
of a Mountie

Early in 1961 I chose to apply to the Royal Canadian Mounted Police for employment and my application was accepted. In joining the force, I may have become the first family member to serve in uniform since 1750 and possibly long before that.

My ancestors originated in the Alsace-Lorraine region of Europe, which lies along the Rhine River, an area coveted and constantly fought over by France and Germany. Interestingly, although most of the population was German in language and culture, it had been part of France for centuries. Around 1765 my ancestors and thousands of other farmers were enticed away from their farms by promises of large tracts of fertile land in the Don and Volga valleys of central Russia. Just a few years earlier Catherine the Great, the German princess who had inherited the Russian throne, had discovered that the economy of the impoverished country was being further undermined by its underpopulated agricultural areas where old-fashioned, unproductive farming methods were used. She knew where to find people with farming skills and the will to work and she advertised in European newspapers, primarily in German-speaking areas, to woo experienced farmers to Russia. As the farmers from Alsace-Lorraine were pacifists, she promised them exemption from the Russian military draft system and then helped them with the cost of the long move to her adopted country.

My ancestors were very successful in their new home and after a generation or two considered themselves to be Russian, though they hadn't forgotten their German culture. After nearly 130 years, however, Catherine's promises became a burden to the Russian government and pressure was building to bring this pool of manpower within the reach of the army draft. By the end of the nineteenth century the writing was on the wall: military service was about to become a reality and the majority of these "Russians from Germany" decided to leave the country rather than serve in the army.

In the late spring of 1899 my grandfather John George Scheideman left his wife, pregnant with their eighth child, my father, and headed for the New World on the opposite side of the globe to find a new home. He knew almost nothing about what he would find there, but he feared for his family's safety in Russia, particularly that of his sons who would soon be drafted into the Russian army. He travelled westward across much of Russia and all of continental Europe, mostly by train, in order to cross the Channel to England. In Liverpool he took passage on a ship bound for Halifax and there he boarded a train, which eventually took him to the end of steel at Edmonton. Old family stories tell of him buying horses and a wagon in Edmonton and making his way farther west to buy a farm. As many of the new immigrants of that time arrived with barely enough money to feed and clothe themselves and their loved ones, we believe Grandfather must have come with considerably more purchasing power.

The Origins of a Mountie

On his journey west from Edmonton, Grandfather passed through some of the finest farming land in Canada, especially in the Spruce Grove and Stony Plain districts, but he travelled on until he was about sixty-five kilometres west of Edmonton in the hilly, tree-covered Mewassin district (a Cree word meaning "good hunting") where other "Russians from Germany" were settling. Just a little north of the North Saskatchewan River's most northerly point and sixteen kilometres to the south and east of White Whale Lake (now called Wabamun Lake) he purchased a farm that had been previously homesteaded by another family. Many theories have been advanced as to his reasons for this choice, ranging from temporary insanity to the more likely one that he chose a parcel of land very similar to the one in Russia where he had grown up and begun raising his family. It was safely above the river's high-water summer flood mark, but it had another feature that must have had a large influence on his decision: passing right through the middle of the farm was a creek that was fed by several

An old native hunting ground and former home to a North West Company trading fort in the 1780s, my father's homestead—and the place I was born—is 65 km west of Edmonton, Alberta.

springs, thereby ensuring a year-round water supply. There was also a house along with several other log buildings, which would serve until he could construct something better.

It was summer by the time Grandfather took possession of the farm and he immediately began cutting and storing hay so he would have feed for cattle and horses. He also cut and hand-hewed logs with an adze and a broad axe to have materials at hand to make additions to the house and other farm buildings. Meanwhile he had sent word back to his wife and family in Russia to tell them to join him, and shortly after my father was born on January 29, 1900, Grandmother and her six sons and two daughters began their move to the other side of the world. My grandmother and the many other women who were in charge of this adventure must have been the type of ladies who could hunt grizzly bears with a stick. In her favour was the fact that the oldest of her children was now about sixteen, and young people of that era were considered adults at a much earlier age than today. By twelve they were expected to accept responsibilities and contribute to the family's fortunes. Child labour laws and rights advocates were still a long way into the future.

Grandmother and her brood made their way from central Russia to England and waited for passage to Halifax on the next available ocean-going ship. Though neither she nor any of her children spoke a word of English, she had to be positive that she and her charges boarded the right vessel. Their Atlantic crossing may have been accomplished in less than ten days and in Halifax she made arrangements to board a train for the final leg of the journey to Edmonton, a distance of almost five thousand kilometres. The longest delay of the whole journey took place at Edmonton because there was no communication with the farm. It was several weeks before word got to Grandfather and he made his way to Edmonton with horses and a wagon to bring them to their new home.

The Origins of a Mountie

While my grandparents and the many other Germans who had moved from Russia to this area north of the North Saskatchewan River were illiterate, they realized that the changing world required educated citizens. It was decided that they must have a school and each family pledged money or hours of labour to that end. The White Whale School was built on a site five kilometres northwest of the Scheideman homestead in the centre of the Mewassin settlement. It opened for its first classes in 1904 and during the next few years adults also attended to learn a few basics of reading and writing and enough arithmetic to be able to keep track of their limited funds. They were also there to set an example for the younger students.

One of the earliest teachers was Mr. Martin Luther Hoffmann. I remember my father talking fondly of him and how he had taught in a way that would make his lessons as interesting as possible. Mr. Hoffmann left the White Whale School and the community in 1917 but the school had thrived during his time there and there was no turning back. The original schoolhouse was destroyed by fire in 1947 but it was rebuilt immediately with resources from the then much larger school district. I also attended White Whale School for a short time prior to its closure in 1956; after that, all the students from the area were bused to the neighbouring communities of Duffield, Stony Plain and Keephills.

Around the turn of the century when my grandparents arrived in White Whale, there was a very enterprising Scottish man living in Edmonton who had grand visions for the future of the city and the country along the North Saskatchewan River. John Walters was a boat and scow builder who also built and operated the first ferry across the river in Edmonton as well as several steam-powered boats that plied the river upstream as far as Rocky Mountain House, a distance of about 320 kilometres. As his business grew he began logging along the banks of the river to supply his factory with raw materials. The Scheideman family worked for the Walters enterprises, cutting stacks of cordwood to fuel the steam boats. During the long and very cold winters, they stacked the wood along the riverbank for easy access by the boatmen even though leaving it that close to the river meant that the product of a whole winter's hard work was in danger from the annual spring floods when the water level could rise by several metres in a single day. A deck of cordwood or logs that had not been sold and floated away by mid-June would almost certainly be lost to the floodwaters.

The Scheideman family did well on their new farm, but during the influenza outbreak in early 1918 Grandfather, his oldest son, John, John's wife, and their two sons all died in the span of one week. By that time the next four sons had all taken up farms of their own within the district and the three youngest sons (one more had been born after the family arrived in Canada) did the same in the years that followed. Philip, the sixth-born son, farmed the original place after Grandfather's death. Katherine, one of the two daughters in the family, married a local farmer and her sister married and raised a family in Stony Plain, about thirty kilometres away.

The family members were a thrifty bunch who worked diligently toward improving their lot in life. The brothers became the owners of the first two steam-powered farm tractors in the district, and these machines became vital to the efficient clearing and breaking of new land so that they were able to expand their holdings. Along with steam power came threshing machines, and the brothers worked well into the winter each year threshing grain on many neighbouring farms. They were proud people who had come to the New World looking only for the opportunity to apply their skills and gain from their hard work.

The Canada Goose

This story begins in 1957, my last year at Stony Plain Memorial High School. I had no idea what I wanted to do with my life so mother pushed me toward the academic program to leave the door open to higher education. The Alberta high school matriculation program of that era required some optional courses and I had chosen to take woodworking as one of my options. My major project during that last year was the construction of a boat. A special order at the local lumber yard provided the necessary two sheets of one-quarter-inch, marine-grade plywood, four feet by fourteen feet. The final result was a twelve-foot V-bottomed boat with a five-foot beam and a good high gunwale. The plan I was using called for a maximum fifteen-horsepower outboard motor but that would be a problem for another day.

Around the last day of school, my brother Don brought the family farm truck to the school and we loaded the boat for the trip home. Later as we unloaded it into the machine shed, we began to plan how we would gather the money for an outboard motor. In those days people seldom bought anything they could not pay for on the spot, though some automobile companies were beginning to advertise monthly payment plans and some tragically misguided people were actually going to their favourite automobile dealership, picking out a brand new car and just driving it away. Those of us from good solid farm-raised stock just shook our heads and wondered what the world was coming to.

A few days after we brought the boat home Don made the sixty-five-kilometre trip to the Edmonton stockyards with a truckload of fattened hogs. The night before he went we listened with heightened interest to the hog price news on the radio; the quotes were well above what we had expected. In fact, the hogs took care of the current farm operating costs and there would even be a few dollars left over. After Don off-loaded the hogs, he dropped into Eaton's department store and discovered that they were having a sale on outboard motors. The very best buy of the lot was a Viking brand outboard motor rated at twenty-five horsepower. These motors were the result of an agreement between Eaton's of Canada and the Outboard Marine Corporation, which made the Evinrude and Johnson brands, so this big Viking motor was simply last year's Evinrude model with a different paint colour and the Viking name slapped on it. It was on sale for $325 including the fuel tank, while the only fifteen-horsepower unit in the store was priced at $375 and the fuel tank was additional. The deal on the twenty-five horsepower motor was more than Don could resist and he arrived home with a cardboard box in the back of the truck that looked like it would hold a young piano.

Over the next few days, we spent every spare minute modifying the transom of the boat in the hope that it would withstand the thrust of that big motor. Don was a self-taught welder and a very good one and he designed and fabricated a very strong, but lightweight, steel centre support, which we bolted to the stern of the boat at the point where the keelson met the transom. With some minor additions to the corners where the transom met the gunwale we were ready for the shakedown cruise. We found a couple of paddles and some ugly and uncomfortable but reasonably priced life jackets and we were all set.

The new motor was lovingly placed in the truck box alongside the boat and we headed for Jackfish Lake, which formed part of the border of a cousin's family farm. We thought that this quiet stretch of water would be the best place for the initial test as there was always the possibility of something embarrassing happening. What if the big motor was to sink the back end of the boat? What if the boat foundered on our first attempt to turn it from a straight-ahead course? We were fairly confident these things wouldn't happen but we didn't want any more audience than necessary.

We started out very slowly going straight forward and in a short time we were running at full throttle in a straight line, the wind nearly lifting our caps off our heads. Turns at low speed increased our confidence rapidly and we were soon doing hard turns at near maximum speeds. This thing was going to be more fun than running barefoot in the creek! On my next trip to the city I bought a pair of water skis and for the rest of that summer we had a wonderful time with them. Our greatest regret during nice weather was all the time we had to put into farming.

Our home farm bordered on the North Saskatchewan River about a kilometre and a half southeast of Grandfather's original farm and the bank at that point was about twelve metres high and nearly vertical, but there were a few spots where runoff water had cut some of the earth away. By using these washouts we could make our way down to the water's edge on foot but no conventional vehicle could get up or down, however, the possibility of exploring the river in our new boat was very intriguing so overcoming this obstacle required some thought and planning.

Farm boys are inventive. We took a pair of steel wagon wheels with an axle and bunk attached and fashioned a platform of planks over a long wooden tongue. The platform was to carry the boat, which would be well tied down, and the tongue was rigged with a hitch so we could attach it to the farm tractor with a long steel cable. We pulled this rig to the selected wash in the riverbank and after a bit of shovel work were able to lower the boat on its platform until the platform formed a little dock at the water's edge and the boat could be easily pushed into the river.

The river was too cold for skiing or swimming but the possibilities for exploration were now almost unlimited. The North Saskatchewan River is more than three thousand kilometres long and we figured that most of it could be navigated if we took some spare propellers along to replace those that tried to take a bite out of the rocks in the river bottom. Time was the only limiting factor, and during the late spring and early summer of our second year with the boat we spent every bit of our spare time on the river.

There was, of course, lots of farm work to be done. In August

My grandfather, John George Scheideman, Sr., bought a homestead near the North Saskatchewan River in 1899 and my father, Jacob, homesteaded the land in the foreground in 1919.

1942 our father, Jacob, had broken his back in a farm accident and become a paraplegic. Although he had very limited use of his legs, he struggled with his handicap for the remainder of his life, continually trying to do some task he had not been able to do since the accident but his ability to farm was definitely ended. His two oldest sons, my brothers Lorne and Don, became the farmers while Dad took up beekeeping and gardening. His realm was now the acre of land surrounding the farmhouse, which was sturdily fenced to keep livestock and poultry out. His beehives were in one corner of this yard and the remainder was divided into a garden, a lawn and an orchard of crabapple trees and raspberry canes. He moved slowly and constantly around this area keeping weeds under strict control. His bees were under his constant observation so they always had enough fresh frames to store honey and swarming activity was kept to a minimum. He knew the special traits of each hive of bees: some were docile and he could work with them without problems, while others were very aggressive and he knew he would be stung several times whenever he had to open one of them. The aggressive hives were best dealt with during the hottest part of a clear summer day; it was not a good idea to go near them early or late in the day. On the other hand, the more aggressive and mean-spirited the hive, the more honey it produced. He would laugh and warn others to not go near them: "They're a hard-working bunch and they won't tolerate any interference." Visitors to the farm marvelled at this crippled man sitting on his makeshift stand beside an open bee hive within a cloud of circling bees but Dad often said that a few bee stings made the honey taste sweeter. He lived with his severe handicap for more years than he had lived a normal life and died at the age of ninety-two.

    Dad had grown up along the river where we now played with our boat and each time we explored a new area we would spend some time debriefing with him because he had a great interest in and much knowledge of the ever-changing course of the river. He and his brothers had dug gravel and coal from the river's banks and cut timber from many of the islands within sixteen kilometres of the original family farm. He learned from our findings and we learned about the prior courses of the river from him.

The last week of June always brought the highest water to the North Saskatchewan River. It seemed rather odd to me that all the snow lying on our entire prairie district could melt in the early spring and it would make almost no visible change to the volume of the river. When the snow melt began in the mountain headwaters, however, the river would often rise right out of its normal channel and cause extensive flooding. It was not until much later when my work took me into several mountain districts in British Columbia that I began to understand where all the water came from. Five hundred inches of snowfall was not abnormal in many of the mountain passes and that much snow equals a lot of river water.

One late June day Don and I launched the boat and were running the river for the last time before the high water would end our access for a while. The water was already rising quickly but we decided to go anyway. Our mobile landing platform made this possible because all we had to do was stop the tractor a bit farther from the top of the bank so our temporary dock would be in the right place regardless of the water level. On this day the river water was dirty with a lot of floating wood debris. We used extra caution to avoid contact with any of the larger floating limbs and trees, though we didn't judge them to be a major hazard. We were heading for an area a few kilometres up the river from our launch site because Dad had made some observations about the eventual shift of the main channel in that area. The high water flow would show us where the main volume was being directed past a curve in the river and an island just above it. As we skimmed along, we saw a lone Canada goose standing just at the waterline on a small island.

These geese had endured heavy hunting pressure for many years after the settlement of the Prairies began. Dad remembered seeing geese by the thousands in his earliest years there but the numbers had dropped constantly until it had become a bit of a novelty to see a few during their migration flights through our area. Now that the birds were making a comeback we were quite sure that some would be nesting along the river.

Normally this lone bird would have taken flight as soon as we came into sight but it stood its ground and watched our approach. We then spotted another goose near the first, sitting on a nest at the edge of the rising water. We circled the island carefully until we found a spot that was sheltered from the current, pulled the boat up and walked over to the nest site. As we came closer the gander challenged us, spreading his wings and standing as tall as he could make himself. He honked and hissed until it became clear to him that we could not be bluffed. He then turned back toward the nest and he and his mate reluctantly took flight. They circled and watched us as we examined the partly flooded nest and we could hear despair in their calls as they passed over us.

The nest held five eggs. They were still warm from the body heat of the goose but the bottom of the nest and eggs were wet with river water. We picked up the eggs, wrapped them in a jacket, headed for the boat and hurried home. Our first stop in the farmyard was the chicken house where we checked the nesting boxes and were very pleased to find a laying hen that had gone into the brooding cycle. This was a common problem with laying hens at that time of year: they would stop producing eggs but they stayed in the nest boxes intent on hatching some chicks. Our selected broody hen clucked and pecked at us as we came near; a sure sign that she was well into nest-warming mode.

We chose a nest box at one end of the rack, added some

dry hay and wood shavings to improve the insulating effect, then placed the five goose eggs into this modified nest and moved the broody hen onto them. The little hen was perturbed but she immediately adopted the new nest and its monster-sized eggs. It was a strange sight indeed: a three-pound Leghorn sitting atop a clutch of eggs that likely weighed more than she did. When we checked again about an hour later, we found the little hen had spread herself to the maximum in an attempt to cover her adopted eggs.

    A week went by and we could wait no longer. Although we had been checking the nest frequently, there had been no sign of change so after dark we returned to the henhouse with a flashlight. Light would not pass through four of the five eggs, indicating that a gosling was growing in each of them. The fifth egg allowed light to glow freely through it and it was obvious that for some reason this egg had not developed. We removed it, allowing the little hen to deal with the remaining four. Then just before we left her to her work, we listened carefully to each of the remaining eggs and to our great joy we could hear a slow rhythmic tapping in each of them. The goslings were beginning their struggle to break the shell and emerge into the world.

    The next evening we found a small cracked area on two of the eggs and we could see movement underneath it. A family conference resulted in the eggs being taken from the nest and brought into the house where they were kept warm with a light bulb in an improvised nest within a cardboard box. The poor old broody hen was left to once again find her niche in the henhouse flock.

    Over the next two days four healthy and very cute goslings joined our family. Dad doted on them in their little cardboard box, checking them regularly to be sure there was food in their crops and that they would take a drink of water if their beaks were dipped in it. He fed them a commercial chick-starter product and lots of freshly picked clover from our lawn. Within a couple of days all four had cleared their digestive tracts of albumin and their clover and chick-starter diet became obvious in their frequent droppings.

The following day brought their first trip to the outdoors. Dad moved himself and the four goslings slowly to the door and out into the yard. He selected a sunny area where there was good grazing for the goslings and the five of them spent several hours getting to know and understand each other. From that first outing it was obvious that one of the goslings was more outgoing and aggressive than the other three and Dad was convinced—and later proven correct—that the new family consisted of three geese and one gander.

For the next few weeks wherever Dad worked in the yard the four geese were nearby and they soon learned that each time he put a shovel or a hoe into the rich black earth he would dislodge some delicious earthworms. This activity brought out the aggressive and pushy nature of the gander and Dad had to exercise care that this fellow did not get all the worms. The more demure geese soon learned to grab a tossed worm and run while they swallowed it but their running was always in a circular pattern because they did not feel comfortable if they were more than a few feet from Dad.

At night the geese were placed back in their cardboard box and brought into the house but they often became anxious in the evenings when we were all sitting around talking. One or more would start peeping and calling and soon the foursome would be in full chorus. The only way to stop them was for Dad to have a little talk with them and to assure them that he was nearby and that everything was in order. Once we had put out the lights and gone to bed, they would remain quiet until morning.

This arrangement was short-lived. After the first week Mom began to mention the obvious odour and shortly into the second week she issued the order for the geese to learn to live outside. A temporary pen with a little roof was made against the house right under the window where Dad spent most evenings. The geese adapted quickly to their new living arrangements; they could hear Dad's voice through the window and therefore everything was okay with them. The green deposit on the ground was easily picked up with a shovel and buried nearby to improve the next vegetable crop.

    They grew at a rapid rate and by their seventh week of life they were in near-adult plumage and would have been flying if they had been raised in the wild. However, Dad had given a lot of thought to these creatures and what the odds of their survival would be if they were allowed to return to the wild. He concluded that without their natural fear and well-deserved mistrust of man, they would all be shot before they could begin their migratory flight. With this in mind, he snipped off the tiny flipper from the end of one wing on each of them when they were less than a week old. They would never be able to fly more than a few yards.

    The geese soon outgrew their need to be penned and sheltered at night and were given free run of the house yard and learned to explore it even without Dad in attendance. Whenever they had eaten their fill and wanted to relax and digest they would move close to the house and sit beneath whichever window that they could best hear his voice. As long as they were able to exchange a bit of information with Dad everything was great in their world. On rainy days when he was confined to the house we could always tell from outside which room he was in by where the geese were located.

    Our mail was left in a metal box at the head of our driveway almost a kilometre from the house but the geese would gladly accompany whoever set out to collect it. They had difficulty keeping up with us if we set a fast walking pace but whenever we had time to adjust to their speed and goose-walk all the way to the mailbox and back they would make the task very enjoyable through their constant talking to us and to each other. Of course, frequently we didn't have time for a complete goose walk but they would be obviously disappointed if they were not allowed out of the yard to accompany us. As a result, they soon learned to scurry along behind as best they could and at about the halfway point on the route they would sit down in close formation and wait for us to get the mail and return. They would greet us when we came back as if we had been away for a week and then would fall into formation for the short walk back to the yard. If Dad was in the yard on their return, they would run to him with their wings extended and immediately tell him all about their little trip.

Their first fall arrived and with it came the south-bound flights of wild Canada geese. Our adopted geese would hear the calls of the migrating flocks and call to them as they passed, however most of these flocks were high in the air in their well-known V formations and there seemed to be little if any acknowledgment or exchange from these passersby. Occasionally a low-flying flock would come by and there would be very obvious talk and excitement between those on the ground and those in the air but the wild birds were too cautious to land close to human habitations and our geese could not join them as they obviously felt inclined to do. Some of the low flyers would land on the river where they felt safe and then make several flights over the yard to try to talk our geese into joining them. These visitations would last anywhere from several hours to a couple of days before the wild flock would abandon their quest and continue on their migratory route.

Had we been inclined to hunt geese, our earthbound birds would certainly have drawn the wild ones into shotgun range and sure kills but we had never shot at wild geese even before our encounter with these near family members and certainly none of us could do so after that experience. This non-goose shooting policy had been started by Dad who told us of observing geese landing in his grain fields where they fed in a dignified and orderly manner. By examining their feeding areas after the birds had left he realized that they picked up nearly every kernel of grain that fell to the ground. They took only what they needed. Wild ducks, on the other hand, would go into a feeding frenzy in a grain field and leave the ground covered in shelled grain kernels. This grain was beyond recovery and farmers developed a dislike for ducks based on the belief and observation that they wasted ten kernels for every one they ate. As a result, most farmers shot ducks whenever they had time and many would invite hunters onto their fields to deter duck feeding.

    The migration time was soon over and the cold weather arrived. We set up our geese in a stall in the barn with straw bedding and feed and water. The barn was not heated by anything more than body heat from the animals that were housed there but the temperature stayed above the freezing point in all but the most severe weather conditions and the geese seemed to thrive. We ensured that they always had an ample supply of grain and water and provided fine gravel or grit to enable them to grind their food in their digestive systems. On every warm winter day they were allowed outside to exercise and see the world. Their first activity on these warm days was to go to the house to talk to Dad about their experiences. He, too, was very much shut in during the prairie winter but he would spend time outside on the warmer days and there would be much discussion between him and the geese. Unfortunately, the brief sunny intervals ended very quickly and Dad would have to return to the warmth of the house while the geese voluntarily returned to their quarters in the barn.

    When spring began to show and the snow melted on the south side of the farm buildings, the geese would come out, have their little visit with Dad and then enjoy the daylight hours playing in the puddles that were sheltered from the cool wind. If the weather allowed they would stay out overnight but they returned to the barn whenever winter attempted a comeback. Then finally spring pushed winter aside and the geese took up residence in the house yard again. All four were fat and sassy. They obviously enjoyed the first sprigs of new plant growth though we still provided grain to supplement their diet. They made no attempts at nest building or egg production that summer because Canada geese do not reach maturity until the start of their third year of life. Instead, the four enjoyed their routine activities with their favourite person and all was well.

It was in the early summer of that first full year with the geese that a provincial conservation officer called at the farm to tell us that someone had reported that we were keeping wildlife in captivity and it was his duty to investigate. This gentleman would, of course, not tell us who that "someone" was but we had our theories about the who and why of the matter. Of course, the law clearly forbade the keeping of wild creatures in captivity and we were fully aware of that fact. We were definitely in violation of this statute and the matter had to be dealt with. Dad wisely chose to level with the conservation officer in the hope that some degree of compassion was available. We told him of finding the flooded nest and our realization that there was no possibility of the geese hatching and surviving in the wild. We also admitted that we knew of the regulations prohibiting keeping wild birds or animals. Dad struggled out into the yard and demonstrated the bond that had developed between him and the geese by feeding them from his hand and talking to them and the geese talked back to him. Then Dad looked the man in the eye and declared that there was not a chance in hell that these geese would ever be used as living decoys to lure wild birds into shooting range. He said, "I hope you can see that I could never condone the shooting of these magnificent creatures." After about two hours the conservation officer left the farm, but before leaving, he told Dad that he would do whatever he could to create an exception in this case, though he could not offer any assurance that he would be successful. We heard no more from the officer or his office.

When later in my life I became a law enforcement officer, this story came to mind on many occasions. Laws are necessary to govern a society and must be enforced, but no matter what circumstances brought about the passage of a law in the first place, there are times when the letter of that law needs to be bent to fit the case at hand, when common sense and compassion must be applied. To my mind, my father and his geese were that kind of situation.

The spring of their third year arrived and things began to change. The gander became a little more aggressive. He would make the kind of threatening moves his father had demonstrated the day we found the river nest but it was obvious that he had mixed feelings about this new behaviour and he seemed to want to apologize after each outburst. His three sisters engaged in nesting activities, picking up bits of dry grass or leaves in their bills and holding them for a brief time and then reaching around to either side and dropping them on the ground behind them. The nesting and aggressive behaviours continued throughout that spring but there was no actual nest building that year nor were there any eggs produced. There was also no mating or even an attempt at mating among the siblings and we all thought of this as another miracle of nature.

Don and I continued boating on the river over those years and we could see that the local populations of wild Canada geese were continuing to grow in spite of the nest losses from the high water. We also noticed that some pairs of geese were establishing their nests in trees, something neither of us nor Dad had heard of or seen before. As the geese were always among the first wild birds to start nesting, they had first choice of location and all the tree nests we observed were on top of magpie or crow nests from

The Canada Goose

previous years. We were unable to get a close look but obviously the geese had carried a lot of new material up to the platform provided by the former tenants.

I still clearly remember when we saw the first goose sitting on one of these tree nests. My brother and I were both inclined to pretend we had not seen the goose head and neck sticking up from the nest because we both thought this was impossible. *Maybe if I don't say anything, it will disappear,* I thought. We did, however, exchange glances, at which point the sighting had to be acknowledged. We slowed the boat and circled near the nest tree and that's when we saw the gander standing on the ground near the base of the tree. We had learned something new about these birds.

We wondered about the young getting to the ground from these nests but obviously they were able to do it. Over the years we had seen tree-nesting ducks and I had been fortunate to be nearby when a hatch of little ducks were making their way into the world from a nest high in a hollow tree. The mother duck stood on the ground at the base of the tree calling to the little ones and in response to her calls the young ducks kept jumping toward the opening above the nest. Each time one was able to reach the hole, it immediately stepped off into the air, flapping its tiny wings and running at top speed as it fell to the ground. Every one of them hit the ground and immediately ran to join its mother nearby. We concluded that the tree-nesting geese must use the same method.

The increased goose population along the river added to our farmyard activity. Starting in the early spring, the river geese would stage frequent close flights and there would be great discussions between those on the wing and our yard-bound pets but the wild birds would not land in the farmyard. They frequently landed in the field between the farmyard and the river, however, and on these occasions our geese would press against the fence and long discussions would take place on a great variety of topics. During these meetings and talks one of the wild young ganders fell in love with one of our farmyard beauties. Although the wild flock would fly back to the river, this love-smitten gander would stay behind and make small talk with his new friend. Our pet goose was also very much into this new relationship. She would stay close to the fence and bat her eyes at her suitor while the other three would go about their business in other parts of the yard. The love-struck gander became quite bold and when he realized that we were not about to do him any harm he began coming right up to the fence so the two of them could actually touch bills. Sometimes he would land on the roof of the farmhouse and stay there for hours but he could not seem to bring himself to land in the confined space of the yard. This restricted courtship carried on throughout that spring and summer and culminated in the early fall with the wild gander landing inside the yard in the very early hours of daylight. After that his early morning arrivals and departures were accompanied by much clamour and we were often awakened by this activity but his wild nature forced him to leave at the first sight or sound that indicated someone was up and around in the farmhouse.

  The wild gander remained after all the fall migration flights had passed over our farm and he continued to make frequent visits to our yard and the love of his life. Then one day, right after the first cold storm of early winter, he was gone. We were concerned that he had come to some untimely end but with the first signs of spring thaw he returned. It was a memorable occasion. There was extreme excitement in the calls and talk from our yard birds and from the wild fellow as well. This time he came right into the yard and all four of our birds greeted him with extended wings and wagging necks. He had been missed and they let him know about it. The strange courtship was now renewed.

  Starting in the third year of their lives on the farm the three geese began to lay eggs. Each of them would make a nest at some carefully chosen place in the yard and lay four to six eggs. None, however, were fertile and by waiting until the goose began to brood the eggs before taking them away we soon learned that she would not usually start another clutch of eggs. Had the eggs been removed each day as they were laid, the goose would continue producing well into the summer. Meanwhile, the wild gander visited daily but there was no mating activity and this fact still remains a mystery. Obviously they had a great attraction to each other but something in their unnatural circumstance prevented mating. Dad had a theory that in nature they would fly together on their migration and this huge undertaking would somehow cement their relationship.

Each spring for four years the wild gander returned, but when the spring of the fifth year arrived, he did not come back. Something had happened to him during the migration. Perhaps his loss of fear of humans had resulted in him being an easy target for a hunter or he may have become the victim of one of the many natural predators he would encounter on each migration trip.

The four geese lived on our farm for seventeen years, gradually gaining access to the unfenced area of the farm and travelling freely within a half-kilometre radius of the farmyard. They always returned by late afternoon to eat the grain that was set out for them and to spend the night inside the garden fence. It was a midsummer day of that seventeenth year when only one goose came back to the yard from their daily excursion. A thorough search of the usual area of their travels revealed nothing. We assumed that if a predator had taken them, there would have been a lot of feathers in the area of the attack but not a trace was ever located. Another theory was that they had made their way to the riverbank and something had startled them and they went over the bank but were unable to get back up.

The farm was a saddened place. The remaining goose was

obviously lonely but after that she would not leave the yard even though the gates were nearly always open. Mother and the goose would make the walk to the mailbox together about twice a week. The passage of time had taken its toll and the lone goose now had much less difficulty keeping pace during their walks. The two of them frequently paused to wait for each other and would often stop to relax for a few minutes together. They truly enjoyed each other's company.

The lone surviving goose became an auxiliary watchdog for the farm, a task that all four geese had always shared, but the survivor now greatly refined the job. She was on duty around the clock and when an unfamiliar vehicle or person arrived she brought them to our attention, honking and calling excitedly. Her ability to identify people and vehicles was amazing. If one of the farm people came onto the home place with an unfamiliar or new vehicle she would sound the alarm and continue to do so until she had identified the occupant. Then as she gradually calmed down, she would give us a piece of her mind for having caused her such unnecessary concern. The reverse situation also applied; if a stranger drove the family tractor or any other familiar farm vehicle into the yard, she remained quiet because she recognized the vehicle but when she realized there was a stranger at the controls she would fly into a total frenzy of honking and calling that we were quite sure contained a great variety of expletives. Fortunately, such incidents were rare! There was always a dog on the home farm and the two seemed to rely on each other to police the area, though the goose was always the first to sound the alarm and the dog would then attend to the required additional investigation. They were not the best of friends but they learned to tolerate each other and worked very well as a team.

It was during mid-summer of the twenty-first year after the arrival of the geese in our lives that the remaining goose disappeared as mysteriously as the other three had. She had been busy around the yard and seemed completely normal right up to the day she was last seen. A search of the surrounding area revealed no trace. A very interesting era had come to an end.

Police Training

As a typical Alberta-raised farm boy, my first years were lived in the sheltered environment of a mixed farm that was too far from the nearest village to get there without one of my folks along. After high school I worked at a variety of jobs from building cattle fences to operating earth-moving machines on road-building jobs. One day in the spring of 1961 I was sitting on a hot, noisy, bad-smelling piece of road-building equipment when I saw a clean, quiet car drive by. It was black with white doors and it was occupied by two young guys in neat and clean uniforms. The sight of this car and its occupants led to some thoughts that had not crossed my mind prior to that day.

The very next time a prairie rainstorm shut down the road construction job, I forced my old car down the mud road to the gravel road and then onto the narrow paved highway leading to Edmonton where "K" Division of the RCMP was headquartered. I approached the front desk with mud up to my ankles and determination in my heart. A senior man with some decorations on his uniform was called to the front desk to deal with me. He looked me up and down and asked where I lived. When I gave him my rural address, he immediately demanded to know why I had not gone to the Stony Plain detachment. I tried to tell him that I had assumed I would be sent to Edmonton in any event but he did not want to hear that. I was told to apply in my hometown and sent on my way.

The process went very quickly after my first visit to the local detachment. I completed numerous forms and documents and wrote an exam and then appointments were made for me to have medical and dental examinations. By then I was beginning to have second thoughts but I had been trained by my parents to complete whatever I started and then face the consequences. Within six weeks of my first visit to "K" Division, I was back there to be sworn in as a regular member of the RCMP and posted to "N" Division in Ottawa.

My family had reservations about what I had done, to say the least. Our family and all those who came to Canada with them had become proud Canadians but a large part of their reason for leaving Russia was the strong possibility that their sons were about to be drafted into the army. While the RCMP was a long way from the Russian army, it was still a uniformed force with extraordinary powers and I was about to become the first of our entire clan to wear a uniform.

Since I owned a car I decided to drive to Ottawa rather than take the train as the people at the personnel office had suggested. Three days of hard driving took me from Edmonton to Ottawa and by the time I got there I had a better understanding of how big our country really is. By the time I arrived at "N" Division barracks, fifteen members of my troop were already there and over the next seven or eight days the remainder of our full count of thirty-two drifted in from every corner of the country. Two were unilingual French from *la belle province*. Those were some very

In Ottawa, 1962, I was a young and eager policeman in dress uniform for the first time.

interesting times as we met and assessed our new troop mates.

Life at "N" Division was an experience that I shall never forget. One of our thirty-two troop-mates felt that he was in way over his head. He was very ashamed but he would sit on the side of his bunk for long periods of time with tears streaming down his face. The site of this tragic fellow was certainly not good for the morale of the remainder of us but I could certainly identify with his loss of control and I suspect there were quite a number of us who were not far off his situation. On about the fifth day this fellow wiped away his tears and announced that he was going home. A group of us immediately surrounded him and delivered a very strong message that he should pull himself together and tough it out at least long enough to have an understanding of where he was and what he was doing. He reluctantly agreed and promised us he would give it a better try.

The first day after our entire troop had arrived and assembled, we were taken by bus to the RCMP stores in Ottawa where we were issued complete uniforms from Stetson hats to long boots and spurs and everything in between. We came back to barracks like a bunch of kids on Christmas morning but we soon learned that along with all of this equipment we had taken on a huge responsibility. The maintenance of our uniforms and appearance was an integral part of the motto of the force—*Maintiens*

Police Training

Le Droit—and it was not an easy task. Over the next weeks we gained more knowledge about the uses and application of leather and brass polish than we had ever dreamed existed.

It was within a week of our uniform issue day that we came into the barrack room to find our tearful troop mate stuffing his uniform into bags and boxes. His suitcase was packed and closed and his home-bound railway tickets were attached to the suitcase. Without a word to any of us he had gone to the administration office and resigned. We were then a troop of thirty-one.

Over the next months we endured a harsh routine. We learned to handle, ride and groom horses. We learned foot drill, physical training and swimming and there were many hours of classroom work in a variety of subjects. During the foot drill and physical training sessions we were often reminded of our missing member. Whenever one of us made a misstep our instructors would suggest that we should make the force a better place by joining the quitter. We quickly developed a thick skin for these abuses, an outer layer that would serve us well as we experienced police life where "the rubber meets the road."

We learned to work together like a well-oiled machine. Whenever one of us was having difficulty with any aspect of the training regimen the rest would come to his assistance, making sure that his difficulties were overcome by whatever means were necessary. We were not all the best of friends but we learned to stick together and to work as a unit in almost every situation. A mistake by any one of us was a mistake by the troop. At the final parade marking the end of training, our troop put on a display of precision foot drill manoeuvres that lasted for thirty minutes without commands. I came away from Ottawa in excellent physical condition but I had an altered point of view: I was now firm in the knowledge that no person or organization would ever put me through such a grueling trial again. To this day I believe I could still recognize the tonsils of several of the instructors but there would be no mistaking those of Corporal E.B. Young.

Although our training days were severe and demanding, they were not tough enough to keep a bunch of young Canadian boys away from the bounty of beauties to be found around the many government offices and businesses in Ottawa. As a result, I came away from there with a problem: I could not get one of these beauties out of my mind and she became my wife about three days after I had reached the minimum service required to be married. We are still enjoying that situation today.

Some days are diamonds: Patricia and I met during my training days in Ottawa and exchanged vows shortly after I reached the minimum service required to be married.

A Training Experience

I had been in the Royal Canadian Mounted Police training academy in Ottawa for about six months when I began to experience a nagging pain and swelling around the back molars on both sides of my upper and lower jaws. I tried to make it go away by ignoring it but time only made the problem worse so I reluctantly joined the early morning sick parade at the administration building. Medical treatment for all regular members of the RCMP was totally covered by the employer so there was no need to worry about the cost of treatment. My concern was that the required treatment would be painful and slow to heal and I might miss some important part of the training schedule. Sadly my expectations about the pain and slow healing were nowhere near the reality of it.

Our medical coverage was administered by the federal Department of Veterans Affairs (DVA) and because there were a great number of us in Ottawa along with many members of the military, there were doctors and nurses in full-time employment to look after all our health issues. Every weekday morning a DVA medical doctor and a nurse attended at our training facility to deal with the sick parade so the next morning I waited along with a few others until I was ushered in to see the doctor. I explained my painful problem. He took a quick look into my mouth and said that the problem was obvious. I needed my wisdom teeth pulled. In his report he wrote that full extraction was required.

After that, things happened with amazing efficiency. The attending nurse made an immediate telephone call and I was told to report to a dentist in the DVA medical facility in downtown Ottawa within a few hours. At the clinic I was shown into an office where X-rays were taken of the affected areas of my jaws. I was then moved to another dental chair where I waited a few minutes before a man in a white smock came in and introduced himself as the dentist. He was a middle-aged fellow of slight build and somewhat shorter than average and he exuded an abundant and obvious odour of liquor. He appeared to be in a trance as he gazed at the newly presented X-ray films for what seemed a very long time. At last he slowly turned and peered into the back of my mouth, leaving me with the feeling that he was examining something that he had not seen for a very long time. His proximity during this visual inspection made the liquor smell almost overwhelming for me.

Then, pivoting slowly toward his assistant, he requested a supply of anaesthetic, which was immediately handed to him, and he proceeded to load a syringe directly within the scope of my vision. The needle on this gruesome tool appeared to be about half-an-inch thick; it was very long as well. Next he turned his attention to my face, placing a small jack (I believe dentists refer to this tool as a spreader) between my teeth at the side of my mouth and ratcheting the thing with a few loud clicks until my jaw was forced open far beyond what I had ever experienced before. While he was making these preparations, he explained that

A Training Experience

his plan was to deal with the upper teeth first and then he would go for the lower teeth. I did not find much comfort in this information but I assumed the uppers must be the more difficult ones to do and the lowers would no doubt be a piece of cake.

He then went about the freezing process, pausing a few times to reload his weapon and driving his needle into more spots around my upper teeth than a wildcat oil drilling crew on the Alberta prairies. When the process finally came to an end, he announced that the freezing would need a few minutes to become fully effective and left the room. He returned a few minutes later with a stronger liquor smell and (thankfully) a somewhat steadier hand. Now he spread an array of tools on a handy glass tray, the most obvious of these being an assortment of pliers and pincers (forceps) far more abundant than I would have needed to overhaul a combine.

I had been peering into mirrors during the previous weeks to get a look at the painful area. I knew that one of the teeth was completely erupted through the gum tissue, two others were partly so and the fourth was only an inflamed bulge of the gum. As soon as Doctor Overproof began the awful procedure, I realized that he was starting with the only fully erupted tooth of the lot. The *!+#!! had chosen to start with the easy one.

Except for his pliers slipping off the tooth and banging hard into the opposite lower tooth on several occasions, this first tooth was on the tray in only an agonizing part of an hour. His next target being somewhat more difficult, he held an extremely sharp-looking tool up in front of my face and stared at it for a long moment. I expected him to test the edge with his thumb but he did not (at least not where I could see it). Instead, he then lurched toward me and began an all-out assault on the second tooth but as the anesthetic was still doing its job I could only partially feel the hacking and slashing that was going on to expose the tooth. Finally setting aside his bayonet he groped through the assorted tools on the handy glass tray and settled on a small tool that looked like a miniature garden spade. With this in hand, he set about tearing away the gum tissue from over and around the tooth. This process went on for a considerable time before he announced to his assistant that the tooth was only partially emerged from the jaw bone, a proclamation that did not fill my heart with jubilation. He placed a small hayrack of cotton packing material over the crater in my jaw and again excused himself. During the few minutes of his absence I made brief eye contact with his assistant; I do not know what the woman saw in my eyes but I was sure I could see pity and despair in hers.

As he returned, Doctor Overproof wiped his mouth with the back of his hand before putting on his mask and gloves again. Now newly refreshed and reinforced he fired up his dental drill and began slashing away at the bone around the remaining upper wisdom tooth. This process went on for a very long time before he set the drill aside and again began groping through the assorted pliers on his tool tray. He selected one with an off-set jaw, sort of tested the heft of it in his hand and again turned toward me. He reached into the depth of my jaw, attached this vicious implement to my unborn tooth and applied a twisting motion to it by putting his upper arm and his shoulder into the job. This action was accompanied by a loud crack, which echoed throughout my body, and an almost overpowering shot of pain. Sweat poured down my face and armpits; the good doctor's assistant wiped away the perspiration from my face but she left the armpits alone. Doctor Overproof had also realized that the anesthetic was wearing off, though I doubt if this fact was quite as obvious to him as it had been to me. Unfortunately, the tooth had yielded only partially to this tactic but had refused to come clear of the bone, and the doctor, after assuring me that we were almost done, asked if I could bear with him for another thrust at the tooth. I foolishly agreed to let him have another shot at it. His assistant brought some small

A Training Experience

triangular objects from a nearby cupboard and he examined these things carefully before selecting one that I believe he placed on the adjoining teeth to act as a fulcrum under his "stump puller." I braced myself as best I could and tried to be prepared for what I feared was about to happen. It came with a crash! Doctor Overproof stood close and a little to one side of me, took a deep breath, bent his knees, squared his shoulders and put everything he had into the next heave. His huge effort resulted in a loud crack and a crunching sound as the roots of the tooth shattered their way out of the bone. This release was accompanied by a shot of pain that made the first one seem trivial. We were only nearing the halfway point of this process and I was prepared to confess to things that I had not even thought of doing.

The completion of the upper tooth extraction required a toast to his success and the doctor again excused himself for a short time. On his return he stuffed cotton packing into the site of his first two excavations and immediately reloaded his anaesthetic weapon in my full view and began the freezing process on my lower jaw. Again he poked and prodded around the back corners of my jaw with his needle, pausing only to reload before immediately resuming the assault. Over the next two hours the torture continued with only short breaks for the doctor to quench his thirst, and as the afternoon wore on, thoughts of self-destruction and surrender alternated in my head with those of revenge and torture. He slashed and drilled and twisted and heaved well into the late part of the afternoon until he had all four large and bloody teeth on his side tray and I was wishing that he would finally find some way to put me out of my misery. Now he produced a wicked curved needle and some twine, threw a few stitches into the excavated areas of my jaws and announced that I was free to go.

For the next four days I lay on my bed in the barracks and slowly regained my strength. I was a regular in the sick parade, needing a fresh supply of pain killers and the ministrations of the attending doctor who removed the numerous bone fragments as they worked their way to the surface of Doctor Overproof's handiwork. Notwithstanding the eventual healing and the relief of the trivial pain that this episode began with, I have never been able to heartily recommend the good doctor or that dental clinic to anyone.

My First Posting

The day of our "Pass-Out Parade" finally arrived. Later we assembled in the gymnasium to be told our postings and I learned that I was to go to Nelson, British Columbia. This news was a great source of amusement among my troop mates because we were all very aware of the bombing and burning being carried out by a group of radical Doukhobors in the Nelson area. My mates laughed and joked about my posting but under the surface I think they were all a little envious because I got the location where things were definitely happening.

I drove across Canada again en route to Nelson. Each night of the trip I bought a copy of the local daily paper and scanned it for the news from Nelson and almost every day another depredation by the Sons of Freedom sect made the front page. On the last night of the trip I stopped in Fernie, British Columbia, and it was there that I read of the bombing of a power line that crossed Kootenay Lake. This line had the longest span of any power line in the world and the damage was estimated at several million

TRAGEDY ON JACKASS MOUNTAIN

The world's longest span of a power transmission line crossed Kootenay Lake until a Freedomite dynamite bomb felled it in April 1962, knocking out electricity to homes and industries for over a month and causing millions of dollars of damage.

dollars, without counting the cost to the homes and industries that would be without electricity for four to six weeks. This estimate was in 1962 dollars when a dollar was still a buck.

The next day I arrived at the ferry that crossed Kootenay Lake within a few kilometres of the downed power line and I drove aboard under the watchful eyes of two members of the force. Two more were on the boat. From the landing site on the west side of the lake I drove the last thirty kilometres to Nelson. The following days were a blur of activity. I was assigned to a roving patrol unit, which travelled the areas where the Freedomite radicals were most active. We checked every vehicle and pedestrian that we encountered during our patrols but found nothing, and although boredom soon set in, I quickly learned every road and trail in the district.

Time passed quickly. I was assigned a variety of duties from guarding the courthouse during trials of the Freedomites

My First Posting

to one-man night patrols where I was required to check every bridge, school, railway track and power line between Nelson and Castlegar and Slocan City. On one of these patrols I saw the bright flash and felt the shock wave from a dynamite blast that had cut off a wooden power pole just across the river from my location.

The attacks by the Freedomites were always a puzzle. There were no clear reasons or excuses for their actions and when asked about their motives they would shrug and say they wanted to separate themselves from all worldly things. Their bombs and fires most often targeted a single power pole but sometimes they would place a few sticks of dynamite at a splice in the railway track. The blast would sever the power pole at ground level or it would destroy two lengths of railway steel and a few wooden ties. Unfortunately, there is always danger when amateurs play with dynamite, though it was obvious that the Freedomites did their best to play their game without causing death or injury to anyone. However, late one night near Castlegar a sixteen-year-old boy

The "bluffs" at Slocan Lake was part of the nightly route I patrolled on BC Highway 6, checking every bridge, school, railway track and power line for sabotage by Freedomite radicals..

was setting the timing device on a homemade dynamite bomb when it ignited. He had been seated in the middle of the back seat of a car, a friend on each side of him and two more in the front seats. The bomb was in his lap. The blast killed him instantly but the other four survived with a variety of injuries plus permanent hearing impairment.

Most of the sect's actions were just plain silly. One night some of them piled a huge amount of dynamite around the tomb of a long-dead leader. The blast could likely have been heard from space. Huge chunks of rock and concrete were torn from the tomb, bits and pieces scattering over a square kilometre of the valley. If the ghost of the deceased leader had been out and about his tomb that night it would have experienced an awful fright. Other than that improbability, the blast accomplished nothing.

And then came the day of the big burn. All of us who were not already on duty were rousted out of bed at about six in the morning. We gathered in the detachment where we learned that the radicals had gone on an overnight shack-burning binge

The smouldering remains of the Doukhobor village of Krestova in 1963 were the former dwellings of the sect's own members. Soon after the burning, the radicals began a march to the Agassiz Prison where many of their number had taken up involuntary residence.

My First Posting

This old gentleman made a valiant effort to save his little greenhouse after his wife—a member of the radical Doukhobor "Sons of Freedom" sect—torched their shack during an overnight burning binge. This is not recommended garb for firefighting.

throughout the West Kootenays, though most but not all of the torched buildings belonged to the sect's own members. The most concentrated burn was at the village of Krestova near the junction of the Slocan and Kootenay rivers. While we knew that many of the Doukhobor people in various locations in the West Kootenay region had sympathetic feelings toward the radicals, we could never be sure of their commitment in either direction. However, if they gave their home address as Krestova, we were certain that they were part of the radical "Sons of Freedom" sect. It was the largest community of known and dedicated radical Doukhobors in the whole region.

On this day my partner and I were sent to Krestova to observe and report on the activities there. As we crested the hill near the doomed village we saw complete destruction. Where there had been about forty shacks in a random cluster there was almost nothing standing. Near the edge of the former village we saw a very old man trying to save his tiny greenhouse from the fire that had taken his shack only a few metres away. He was naked except for a pair of leather boots. In his hands was a garden hose that provided only a trickle of water and it was obvious that he was fighting a losing battle. There were tears streaming down his face as he conceded to the fire. At the other side of the burned-out village was a cluster of naked women. They stood in a half-circle all facing outward with their arms folded as they glared their defiance at us. Inside the semi-circle was a group of terrified children. My partner and I were both single and innocent. Never had we observed such a display. Most of the women could be described as "abundant" and many of them were quite old. Most of their breasts extended well below their folded arms. A bevy of furry critters could also be seen, most but not all situated below the breasts and some only partly visible below a huge belly. All in all, it was an awesome sight.

 Over the weeks following the big burn most of the radicals made a great display of trekking to the jail at Agassiz where many of their number had been sentenced for bombings and burnings. Over the ensuing years as the prisoners were released they were met by their families at the prison gates then drifted away to a variety of locations throughout the province where they took up the pursuit of life along with the rest of us. The Freedomites had finally seen the light.

Jock Straps

Historically, the Royal Canadian Mounted Police had not been British Columbia's police force. Until 1950 that had been the responsibility of the British Columbia Provincial Police, which had its beginnings in the establishment of a constabulary on Vancouver Island in 1849. The Fraser River gold rush of 1858 had necessitated the organization of another police force on the mainland and the two were amalgamated in 1866. When BC joined confederation in 1871, the two units became known as the British Columbia Provincial Police. As the population of the province grew, the regions were divided into policing zones that were established by a simple and effective method: police presence was obviously required in each community of a certain size and by some smaller places in isolated locations. The jurisdiction for the remainder of the territory surrounding these places was decided by natural barriers such as lakes or rivers or mountain ranges. Where there were travel routes between police units the boundaries were set at the approximate mid-point. When the RCMP

The Shoulder Strap had a noble purpose during the history of the BC Provincial Police until the force disbanded in 1950. After that, the magazine only exacerbated the animosity between regular RCMP members and former provincial police officers who were absorbed into the ranks. COURTESY OF THE LANGLEY CENTENNIAL MUSEUM, BRITISH COLUMBIA PROVINCIAL POLICE FONDS MSS 105 took over the policing contract after the provincial police force was disbanded on August 15, 1950, most of these areas of police responsibility were left intact.

While the Lower Mainland area and Vancouver Island had many large and long-standing municipal policing contracts, in the BC Interior only the city of Nelson had its own municipal police force; the remainder of the province's municipalities had been the responsibility of the provincial police. Thus, with the politically motivated takeover of the provincial policing contract by the RCMP, the force was suddenly thrust into the municipal policing business on a large scale, though prior to this they had entered into very few municipal contracts. Policing of places such as Burnaby, Coquitlam, North Vancouver and Surrey were a new venture for the RCMP and many thinkers within the force will still argue that municipal policing was not something that the force was designed for or prepared to deal with efficiently.

Tragically, the contract signed by the force's political masters in Ottawa compelled the RCMP to engage all the former members of the BC Provincial Police who decided to stay in their chosen law enforcement occupation. From a total strength of 520 provincial police, 492 became members of the RCMP by this back-door route and their entire transformation from provincial police to RCMP was deemed to have been accomplished by simply issuing RCMP uniforms to them. In one of Canada's earliest blunders in the art of political correctness, no correctional adjustments in the form of retraining were undertaken. Attempts at retraining by the few senior RCMP members who had been transferred into British Columbia were met with hostility and contempt from the former provincial police and as they were very much the majority in the new provincial establishment, the standards of conduct and behaviour that had become established over the history of the RCMP were about to be severely compromised.

This mass absorption was undertaken in spite of the fact that the former British Columbia Provincial Police had been in a management crisis and corruption had been rampant. In fact, it had been this internal decay that had compelled the provincial government to seek the alternative they found in the RCMP. This politically arranged merger brought a great number of people into the force who would not have qualified for engagement under any other circumstances and the force was to pay dearly over the next decades.

When I arrived in the province in 1962, the senior managers in nearly every detachment were former members of the BC Provincial Police. Fortunately, they were by that time slowly beginning to lose their majority status in the force within BC, though the process was taking far too long. Most still harboured resentment toward the RCMP, even though they had been wearing that force's uniform for twelve years and this resentment was the cause of constant friction between them and the trained RCMP members. This was made worse by the efforts of the former provincial police members to keep the old ways by holding informal gatherings and formal meetings where the regular RCMP members were excluded. These meetings and other questionable conduct created mutual distrust and the establishment of a cohesive police operation was all but impossible.

The animosity was not all one-sided, of course. Over the years of their existence in British Columbia the provincial police had published a magazine called *The Shoulder Strap,* which had proved to be an effective method of keeping their widely scattered membership up to date on police-related matters around the province. Even after the takeover by the RCMP, the former members tried desperately to keep it going. The RCMP members bastardized the title of the old magazine and all former members of the British Columbia Provincial Police became known among us as "jock straps."

In the years after the takeover, many inexperienced new

Jock Straps

members of the RCMP were sent to British Columbia from the training divisions and found themselves being guided and directed by those whose conduct and thinking had brought about the downfall of the former provincial police. As they had been taught to do in training, these young and malleable recruits looked to the senior members with rank and experience for their pattern of conduct. Fortunately, there were some former members of the provincial police who conducted themselves in a very exemplary manner and a new RCMP recruit was indeed lucky to find himself under the guidance of one of these men. This was not, however, the general rule and many new recruits were severely corrupted by what they witnessed and were taught by their new leaders. Examples of undisciplined behaviour and an attitude of entitlement were so commonplace that it almost seemed to be normal and acceptable.

One senior "jock strap" corporal at my first detachment in Nelson had established a routine in connection with the requirement to create a written log of vehicle kilometres and destinations after every patrol. This man walked to work each morning and entered the building through the post garage where the three detachment patrol cars were parked. After walking around each of the cars and checking for damage, he would climb into each car and record the odometer reading in his notebook. He would then go into the office and check the entries in the log books for each of the cars. At a glance, this action appeared to be that of a thorough and conscientious supervisor and no doubt it would have revealed any unreported damage to the cars. Sadly his motive for this attention to duty was not as commendable as it first appeared. On finding a neglected log entry Corporal Jock would enter a patrol in his own name for the previous day. These imagined patrols would always be for the hours around ten in the morning until about two in the afternoon and he would then submit an expense claim for the mid-day meal. Lunch and a tip for the waiter amounted to about one dollar and fifty cents in those days but those were the days when a dollar was still a buck. This man made little or no attempt to hide what he was doing. He had obviously convinced himself that he was entitled to this petty theft by virtue of his job.

He kept his ill-gotten money secreted in a file drawer in the office and he would often brag to the young RCMP members about the amount that he had accumulated over just a few months. Some of us were shocked by this display of poor behaviour but I am sure some others didn't give it much thought and concluded that this was an acceptable practice in the police world. They had, after all, been trained to look up to the more senior members who wore the same uniform as their own.

One morning a man who lived in a rural area came to our front counter to tell us that he had not seen his elderly neighbour for a day or more. He had noted his absence because he frequently saw the old gentleman picking up his mail or strolling around the area where they both lived. Corporal Jock stood nearby while I spoke to the man at the counter and completed the paper record but on picking up the gist of the concern Corporal Jock grabbed a set of patrol car keys and left the office immediately, saying he would attend at the residence and investigate. I thanked the man for bringing this matter to our attention and he left the office.

There was nothing for me to do now except wait for the corporal's findings. The old fellow's residence was about a twenty-minute drive from our office and Corporal Jock soon called by police radio to say he would be ten-seven (off the air) at that location. As all radio messages were recorded in a log entry by our radio room staff to allow close monitoring of the activities of vehicle patrols, I was able to note that it took Corporal Jock forty-seven minutes to determine that the old fellow was dead and that he had likely been that way for at least a day. The radio message came with these words, "Old Mr. Citizen has passed on. God rest his soul. Have Constable Scheideman contact the coroner and official administrator and then attend here to handle this file. It will be good experience for him as he has not dealt with this type of incident before."

One of the duties of the official administrator was to deal with the security of property of persons who died suddenly with no family members immediately available. In this case, the official administrator requested that I pick him up and we would attend the scene together. As we drove up to the residence accompanied by a vehicle from a funeral home, Corporal Jock drove away with a big wave and a smile.

The old fellow had died in bed and it appeared he had simply forgotten to wake up that morning. I recorded the scene with photographs and a measured sketch before the body was removed by the funeral home staff, and the official administrator and I then began the task of listing effects and valuables in the home. The dead man's trousers hung on the back of a chair beside the bed. His wallet and identification papers were in a pocket of the trousers along with a bit of coinage. The well-worn watch pocket of the trousers was empty. The man was a pensioner and would have received his pension cheque only a few days before his death but it appeared he had spent it all in those last few days of his life. Perhaps the old gentleman knew the end was near.

We searched the house for a copy of a will and any valuables that would require removal to safe storage. The deceased had lived there alone for several years and had not spent much time dusting his shelves and cupboards and as a result it became quite obvious to me that nearly everything in the house had been moved very recently.

Later that summer on a Sunday that happened to coincide with my day off, my fiancée persuaded me to attend church. This was a rather new experience for me so I was quite interested in the pageantry of the event. The choir loft was filled with people in black robes who sang beautifully and among the folks in that choir loft I recognized Corporal Jock. After the service he came bounding over to us and invited us to his home for lunch. We had no plans beyond being together so we were not able to avoid the invitation. And the visit was very pleasant. The home of the corporal and his wife had all the appearances of a place of family values and love.

During this visit he took me to his little office-den in the basement where he kept a wonderful collection of valuable trinkets and novelty items. There were pocket watches, pewter steins, silver and gold coins from all around the world and many more small articles. I had no accurate idea of the dollar value of this collection but it had to have been well into the thousands and policemen in those years were not well paid. However, this man was able to support his family very nicely and build this collection as well.

The detachment in Nelson, my first posting in British Columbia, was a fairly large establishment, considering that we were not involved in municipal contract policing. When I arrived, a senior staff sergeant was in charge with two corporals to assist him, and all three of these supervisors were "jock straps," but before my first year was over, in a very sudden order from above, our staff sergeant was transferred to a large municipal contract detachment in the opposite corner of the province and the staff sergeant from that detachment was posted to Nelson. Both had more than enough service at the time to go to pension and there was speculation among us that the move had been orchestrated in the hope that they would elect to take their pensions and make the force a better organization.

Unfortunately, they both chose to accept the transfer and the much needed improvement did not happen. Our replacement

Jock Straps

staff sergeant did not improve our lot in the least. The new man would often fly into a rant about the poor quality of the RCMP and the sorry state of policing in British Columbia since the force had taken over the provincial contract. His rants never disclosed any concrete examples or evidence of poor policing but it was very obvious he pined for the old days of the provincial police and harboured a deep resentment toward the RCMP.

It was less than a year after the staff sergeant swap that a trained RCMP member at the other detachment got himself into trouble through some unacceptable behaviour. I do not recall the exact nature of the investigation that followed but the member involved was facing dismissal from the force and most of us agreed it was for a good reason. The member about to be punted was bitter about his fate, however, and he made it clear to any and all that he would not go quietly. This declaration created waves of terror among nearly all the "jock straps" in British Columbia and the daily rant by our staff sergeant became louder and was joined by a chorus from our two corporals. "What kind of a dirty low-down bastard would blow the whistle on his comrades like this guy's doing?" they asked. Their diatribes were very much like the talk one would expect to hear in a penitentiary after one of the convicts had "ratted to the screws."

After the investigation the disgraced member was dismissed but before he went on his way he provided a great deal of information about the conduct of others he had worked with during his police service. Investigations began into the allegations he had made and they revealed some very unacceptable practices. Unfortunately, these investigations were not all directed at the conduct of former members of the British Columbia Provincial Police. A few fell on the doings of regularly trained RCMP members but the eventual result was an improvement to the basic stature of the organization.

The most memorable of the allegations involved the falsifying of records concerning prisoners' meals at the large municipal detachment with which we had traded staff sergeants and this activity tainted every police officer at that establishment, both RCMP and former provincial police. The city in which this happened was known for its excessive alcohol consumption by both the Native and general populations and drunks were picked up by the hundreds every month. At that time they were still being prosecuted in court under the Liquor Control Act. The necessary paperwork was prepared overnight and they were marched to the court the next morning. The routine fine was ten dollars or, in default, one day in jail but as they had already been in jail for part of the day they were free to go after their hearings. What these drunks did not know was that the records at the detachment indicated they had been provided with both a dinner and a breakfast, though almost without exception drunks were arrested after the evening meal time and they were released without breakfast the next morning. The prison meals were supplied by a small business that consisted of a grocery store and café and the owner was a partner in the conspiracy and received direct payment for the number of meals certified to have been consumed by prisoners. A generous portion of the ill-gotten funds was then distributed to most of the police in that community by way of grocery credits and various other freebies from the store/café.

 A senior "jock strap" staff sergeant—whom I will call Staff Sergeant Jock—from the local regional administration office was put in charge of the internal investigation into the meal scandal that had been outed by the dismissed officer. He worked out of the administration office in the same municipality as the offending detachment, so if he was not already aware of the scam, he should have been. Nevertheless, he was selected and charged with this most difficult and embarrassing investigation. His inquiry revealed that a constable had been appointed from within the detachment to attend to all the accounts and returns that were required at the end of each month. This position, which was a constant day shift with weekends off, was almost completely removed from the day-to-day operations of this large police establishment so the officer who held the job had been free to participate in the fraudulent practice with the meal supplier. This officer, whom I will call Constable Goat, had recently been transferred to a location about 160 kilometres from where I was stationed. The job he was vacating, however, was not the kind that the majority of the young members of that detachment were interested in, despite the attractive work hours, because they had joined the RCMP to be policemen and the opportunity to replace Constable Goat and be a full-time paper pusher held little or no appeal. As a result, a constable from another location in the province had recently been transferred into the position and he had foolishly chosen to carry on with the meal scam. Thus, after these transfers it continued to work as it had been designed until the constable who got the boot blew the whistle.

 Staff Sergeant Jock explored the records in detail and took statements from nearly everyone who worked at or had been associated with the diseased detachment. He then decided he would drive to our location, a distance in excess of sixteen hundred kilometres, to conduct a proper and thorough interrogation of his old comrade who had previously been in charge of the detachment, a man whom I will hereafter refer to as Staff Sergeant Jock 2. His route of travel also took him through the community to which Constable Goat had recently been transferred and en route Staff Sergeant Jock took a room there, arranged a meeting and spent most of a full day interviewing the constable.

 The next day Staff Sergeant Jock continued his drive and arrived in our community. He did not take commercial accommodation, choosing rather to stay at the residence of Staff Sergeant Jock 2. Over the next two days these two no doubt planned, discussed and conducted a very thorough interrogation and investigation and then with his inquiries finished Staff Sergeant Jock began his return trip. A couple of hours on the road took him again to the town where Constable Goat was working and living. He stopped by the residence of the constable and had a rather brief discussion in the police car in front of his home. The staff sergeant then continued his return trip but before he was more than a few kilometres away Constable Goat shot himself with his service revolver. The shot did not kill him but it left him with sufficient brain damage that he could not be called to testify in any hearings about this affair or any other.

Shock and disbelief spread throughout the province. What could possibly have caused this constable to commit such an act? Surely he must have lost his thinking capacity. Those of us who were not involved could only wring our hands and wish he had not been so foolish as to yield to the extreme pressure that we suspected had been applied to him.

The investigation ground on. Staff Sergeant Jock was removed from the file and it was taken over by senior men from other areas of the province. The conclusion of the investigation indicated that Staff Sergeant Jock 2 and the transferred Constable Goat had been the originators of the scam as it stood at that time. There were many indications that a similar but smaller version of the scam had been operating at that location for years before that but no follow-up investigation was undertaken in that regard.

The constable who had foolishly taken over the corrupted desk job was dismissed from the service. Both the detachment commanding staff sergeants were convicted in service court and left the force after having been reduced in rank to the extent that their potential loss of pension left them no choice. No justice was tried or applied in regard to the attempted suicide by Constable Goat.

Salmo's Flying Ace

This story begins in 1949 with the birth of a baby in the community of Creston at the south end of Kootenay Lake. Life was to become a constant struggle for this little fellow due mainly to alcoholism in his immediate family and the complete lack of social support systems in those days, particularly in rural communities. Although he had a bright mind and was physically capable, hunger and a lack of anyone to care about his well-being left him with an anti-social attitude that would continually keep him from enjoying life as others of his generation did.

By the age of twelve he was in constant conflict with everyone in his community and had come to the attention of the police in his hometown on many occasions but nothing seemed to deter his negative behaviour. Then in 1963 he committed a series of break-and-enter offences at businesses and homes that landed him an indefinite sentence at the youth detention facilities at Brannen Lake near Nanaimo. He was now fourteen years old and a very hardened case.

Throughout BC's prison system the old-school disciplinarians were under pressure at that time to make prison life more pleasant for the inmates and to introduce educational opportunities for these unfortunate victims of society. This was particularly the case at Brannen Lake because it was the only youth detention facility in the province. As a result, the rules there had been changed in many ways prior to our young friend being sentenced but they still required inmates to get up at a fixed time in the morning and go to bed at a fixed time at night. Physical exercise was also mandatory and all prisoners were required to wear the same style of prison-issue clothing. Unfortunately, while our young friend from Creston enjoyed having three good meals a day set before him, he rebelled at every other aspect of the controlled lifestyle and on the evening of his tenth day in the correctional facility he gathered his few possessions and simply walked away.

The RCMP were advised of yet another walkaway and made the required entries in their records but such incidents were so commonplace that the police reaction was almost non-existent. A report would be prepared within a few days and within a few weeks the information would be forwarded to every police establishment in the province by way of index cards containing the fugitive's vital statistics and possibly a photograph.

Meanwhile, our friend spent the first few weeks of his new freedom exploring the southern end of Vancouver Island. It was early spring and the weather conditions were fairly good so sleeping outdoors was almost a pleasant experience. He was an accomplished thief by that time but he would never pass up an opportunity to earn a little pocket money by doing odd jobs for anyone who would hire him, so he was able to keep himself fed and clothed as well as he had been at any time in his short life. Because he had no idea how little concern his escape had actually generated, however, he was constantly worried that someone would recognize him and each time he saw a policeman he became extremely stressed. One particular morning while he was working as part of a crew on a daffodil farm, a police car stopped at the edge of the field and two policemen got out and spoke with the foreman of the work crew. The young fellow immediately convinced himself that the cops were there to get him and he struggled with an almost overwhelming urge to throw down his equipment and run. What he couldn't understand was why the police got back into their car and drove off without taking him into custody but he knew very well that they would be back to get him. What else could they possibly be discussing with his crew boss?

As soon as the police car was off the edge of the field he threw down his tools and ran, leaving behind the small amount of money that was owed to him. He went directly to the ferry landing where he paid the fifty-cent foot-passenger fee and made his way to the mainland. Vancouver Island was obviously far too hot for such a desperate fugitive. Over the next month or so he discovered that he could get more farm field work than he wanted to do and he went from job to job, gradually working his way up the Fraser Valley to Hope. He hitched rides over the Hope–Princeton Highway and into the Okanagan Valley where he was again able to find farm work and he settled for a while around Osoyoos.

He had no plan for the journey he was on but he was gradually heading back to Creston, the only home he had known, though he could not think of a good reason why he was doing this. Had he given some thought to returning to that area, he would easily have come to the conclusion that this was a bad plan. There was always the possibility that he would come to the attention of the police regardless of his location but in Creston it would be only a very short time before he was recognized and apprehended. Rational thought was not his long suit, however, and he was lonely for the only community he had ever known. Loneliness was the driving force in his attempt to return there.

Slowly over the next weeks he made his way through Grand Forks and on to Trail and then to Salmo. However, the highway through the Kootenay Pass that would link Salmo to Creston was still under construction and it would be August of the following year before it would open to traffic. He could have gone north through Nelson and taken the Kootenay Lake ferry, which was a necessary part of the only conventional route to Creston, but many of the crew members on the ferries were from his home area and he feared recognition. Instead he hoped to somehow follow the route of the new highway to Creston.

He took the road south away from town along the Salmo River, heading for the western foot of the new mountain highway. He had some basic grocery items with him to stave off hunger for a few days while he explored the possibilities but a few kilometres out of town he discovered the Salmo "golf-port," a long strip of smooth, flat ground lying along the river. This area, covered in nicely mown grass, served as the golf course for the little community but its end-to-end fairways also provided a runway for the few small airplanes owned by local residents. What caught the attention of our young friend was the row of little single-engine aircraft sitting in the open beside the grassy landing strip. Except for his police-escorted plane ride to Brannen Lake, which had thrilled and excited him, he'd had no experience or contact with aircraft and now here was a wonderful opportunity to touch and explore any of the little planes that sat there completely unattended—and unlocked.

He quickly learned a few hiding places where he could stay out of sight when any of the local citizens came to play golf or come and go with their airplanes, and for a couple of days he hung around the planes, getting into them and pretending to fly and sleeping in a pilot's seat during the nights. About the third day he decided he would borrow one of these flying machines and complete his journey to Creston in grand style. He had played with the control sticks in a few of the planes and watched what happened when he pulled or turned the controls and saw how the rudder pedals caused a reaction in the upright part of the tail. With all this new-found knowledge he felt quite capable of flying over the mountains to his final destination, though he had not given any thought to how or where to get his borrowed equipment back onto the ground. He decided that these things could be best dealt with as the need arose so for the time being he would just concentrate on getting off the ground.

He was obviously a bright young fellow with a mechanical ability that he must have been born with since his upbringing had certainly not provided any training or guidance in that area or any other. In a very short time our young flying ace figured out the starting process on his chosen airplane and in no time at all he was taxiing around on the "golf-port." It was early evening and the cooler air would have given the little plane a bit of an advantage, though our friend did not know this—or any other basic facts about flying, for that matter. He made his way to the end of the grassy strip, turned the machine around and opened the throttle wide. The little plane sped along the strip and in almost no time it took flight. In one smooth burst of lift, the new pilot and his craft found themselves high above the trees of the valley bottom. He was so busy experimenting with the controls of the little aircraft that, contrary to being frightened at finding himself aloft, he was quite thrilled with each discovery and pleased with the abrupt responses he received from each experiment he tried with the controls. This was going to be a piece of cake!

He could clearly see the highway and the river below and he knew that Creston lay just beyond the mountain range he could see to the east. The little plane was already flying along parallel to the river valley bottom almost by itself and he could see no reason why it would not also fly along parallel to the side of the rapidly rising surface of the mountains he intended to cross. He turned to the east and held the controls to climb straight over the first of the mountains but the steep climb was more than the little plane could possibly accomplish. The side of the mountain rushed toward the airplane but the new pilot still expected the plane to realize what was required of it and react as he thought it should.

The miracle of this story begins with the unavoidable fact that the little plane had no understanding and no ability to do what the pilot wanted it to do. Still he held the controls in the maximum climb position. The craft slowed continuously, lost the airflow over its wings and stalled at the exact moment that it was about to crash into the mountainside. The nose of the plane dropped like a stone and it came down into a large clump of birch trees, which greatly cushioned the impact. While the aircraft was completely destroyed, the novice flying ace escaped with a black eye and a few minor bruises.

The unusual departure from the "golf-port" had been observed by several people who had watched breathlessly as the new pilot executed his impossible stunt. Two of these witnesses immediately began the climb up to the crash site and were amazed to find a survivor. They ensured that he waited there for the police and the ambulance and he was again taken into custody where he was no doubt dealt with again by the full force and effectiveness of the law.

Born for a Bad End

I have chosen to write this story at the risk of exposing a soft spot in the armour of an old and hardened cop. The events I describe here happened within the first few years of my service. I had transferred to the traffic section and was enjoying the action that this change had produced. I no longer had to work graveyard shift but the four-to-midnight shift often kept me on the job until well into the wee hours of the morning. Vehicle crashes were our unit's main responsibility, and as a rule, if a crash happened after I had left the office at the end of my shift and it did not have unusual complications, the guys on the graveyard shift would take care of it. It seemed, however, that people really liked to cause these events very near the end of my evening shift.

In those years a young person could get a driver's licence at the ripe old age of sixteen based, it seemed, on the belief that everyone had to start somewhere, and the issuing of this licence was almost automatic on the payment of a few dollars and placing a signature on the required forms. The testing of the new driver's skills or any requirement to prove some knowledge and training was still far into the future. Naturally this system produced problem drivers, and the first to come to my attention was a sixteen-year-old boy who had been born and raised in a shack community at the edge of my patrol district. For the purposes of this story I will call him Palmer. He was still considered a juvenile in the eyes of the law so he required a parental signature to get his licence but he managed to convince one of his parents to sign the forms during one of the brief spells when he/she was sober enough to manage the task. Both parents suffered from an insatiable thirst and every minute of their existence was taken up with their desperate struggle to quench this thirst. They existed on funds from the public welfare system because they were unable to find time to work or earn their support by any other means. Palmer had existed in the midst of this situation all his life. He had been an occasional attendee at school during the period that he was required by law to be there and the day he turned sixteen his formal education was complete.

The shack where he and his parents lived was surrounded by a variety of junk vehicles that provided endless possibilities for cobbling together a road runner of some description and out of all these wrecks Palmer somehow managed to put together a vehicle that would actually run. The positive thing about his vehicle activity was that he soon showed himself to be quite adept at patching a great variety of vehicle parts into something that could be forced to run the roads. Had he been provided with even a minimum of guidance and encouragement, he would very likely have been a good addition to the crew at some automotive service facility but the vehicles he built were always a marvel of borderline disaster. Brakes, steering components, suspension parts and tires did nothing toward making the vehicle move so in his mind they were of no importance. No doubt Palmer could have been stealing parts for his variety of vehicles but this activity was not the subject of police reports or certainly not reports that implicated him.

Insurance and licence requirements were of no concern to him and of even less concern were all the safety aspects of vehicles. Therefore, once he obtained his driver's licence he became a continuous problem to the police. Fortunately for him, he was still a juvenile in the eyes of the court and therefore had an abundance of protection from the routine police actions that might have taken an older person off the road almost immediately. Gasoline for his cars was always cheap and available through the use of what we came to call the "Palmer credit card," which consisted of a siphon hose and a container. In a very short time he learned how to make such expert use of these tools without being noticed that we seldom if ever received any complaints from his victims.

It was early in my experience on the traffic unit that I first met Palmer. He was driving one of his junkers, one that had so many visible violations that no policeman could drive by without stopping its driver to have a closer look. While the vehicle itself was remarkable, Palmer's conduct was almost unbelievable: he was verbally abusive and extremely foul-mouthed from the moment I walked up to the side of his car. For a sixteen-year-old he demonstrated an amazing variety of abusive language, which he must have learned from his alcoholic and anti-social parents. (Later I had the misfortune on several occasions to meet Mommy and Daddy on their home turf and this experience clearly showed where Palmer had perfected the art of foul and abusive language.) I was quite taken aback by this first encounter but I soon learned that this was his everyday, routine conduct whenever he came in contact with anyone in authority.

Over the next few months I had numerous contacts with Palmer and each was a very unpleasant event. I told him that it was my job and my full intention to get him off the road just as quickly as I could manage it within the restrictions of the laws governing juvenile offenders. He replied with more verbal abuse and told me that he didn't care what I did. However, I did notice that there was a bit of a break in his voice and I saw that he was close to tears. I took advantage of that moment and invited him to have a meaningful conversation without all the abuse and loud talk. Over the next twenty minutes or half an hour we talked about a variety of things and he told me that he wanted to get away from his home and find somewhere to live on his own. I tried to assure him that he could do that but it would be a struggle made worse by his combative and abusive attitude. Palmer admitted that he was fully aware of the problems his conduct was causing for him but he was so angry at the world in general that he just did not care. Again I could see that he was on the verge of tears but this was very embarrassing to him so I broke off our talk by asking him to try to be less abusive in his inter-personal meetings and see if things would improve for him. Before we parted, I suggested that we should talk again soon and I might be able to put him in contact with someone who could help him to make a new start on his own. He agreed that he might do that but he was obviously very suspicious. Why was I offering to help him?

The following week I was back on the afternoon shift, four to midnight. It was nearing midnight, the shift had been quiet and I had spent a few hours in the office clearing some of the never-ending paperwork. We were interrupted by a telephone call from an excited person who had just seen a vehicle leave the highway and crash down a rocky embankment. The reporting person was quite sure the car had gone end-over-end at least once as it went down the bank from the highway.

One of the other constables ran with me to the patrol car and we raced (code three) over the few kilometres to the crash location. We found a totally destroyed old car at the bottom of the bank and at about the middle of the debris trail we found

Palmer's dead body. He had suffered a massive head injury that left no doubt that he had died very quickly. Another young fellow had been in the passenger seat but he had somehow managed to stay with the car and he had suffered only minor injuries. The ambulance crew loaded the survivor on a stretcher and quickly removed him to medical aid. A second ambulance attended and I assisted with the awful task of loading Palmer's body for the trip to the morgue. It was then my turn to try to hide the embarrassing tears as we struggled up the rocky slope to the highway. Policemen were expected to be much tougher than that.

Death in the Bush

In the years prior to my arrival in Nelson the greatest portion of the "easy logs" had been harvested from the forests of the BC Interior and logging activities were being pushed into previously inaccessible areas where expensive roads had to be built. As there was still great demand for BC forest products, this road building and the much more expensive harvesting of the trees on this tough terrain could be factored into the end cost of the products.

At that time the forest industry was the backbone of nearly every community in the Interior and every community had its share of sad stories where logging operations had taken an unexpected twist and cost the lives of some of the local workers. Many of these stories concerned the men who worked at the front end of the operation as fallers, depending only on their chainsaws, fuel and oil, files and a few tools to keep their saws working throughout the day. These men were subject to all the unexpected things that the wilderness forest had to offer.

Shortly after I arrived in Nelson, I attended a call with our identification specialist to investigate the sudden accidental death of a worker in the remote headwaters area of White Water Creek a few miles south of the city. Today the upper areas of this creek have been developed into a large downhill ski operation that hosts more visitors in one winter day than had entered that valley in several thousand years before my trip there to investigate this tragedy.

We drove in on a recently constructed very steep roadway, which took us up into a beautiful alpine valley. The road ended in a cleared area that loggers call a landing, where the logs are gathered and sorted prior to loading onto trucks for the haul to mills or railway sidings. The area around this landing was still untouched forest except for a few small areas where the logging was already underway.

We were met by a group of men who were involved in various ways with the actual logging and some who were from the BC Forest Service. There was a noticeably subdued atmosphere among them. The foreman of the logging operation directed us to the spot where an experienced faller had been cutting and bucking trees to prepare them for the skidders that would drag them to the landing. This man had worked for many years as a faller and was well known for his cautious approach to his dangerous job but he was also known for his skill and ability to produce a great number of logs per day.

The accident had happened on a steep, tree-covered slope where the ground began to rise sharply toward the mountains. The faller had taken a wedge-shaped cut out of the downhill side of a metre-thick fir tree and had started the cut on the uphill side that would result in the tree tipping down the hillside. He had only cut about thirty centimetres into the tree when for some reason he removed his saw and began moving to the other side of the tree. The steep slope caused him to be very close to the tree and facing it when the tree split vertically upward from the cut he had just made. As the split ran up the tree trunk for more than ten metres, the section of the tree closest to the faller had burst sideways, striking him with such force that it broke nearly every bone in his body. It appeared that he was dead before he fell in a gruesome heap at the foot of the tree. The partially cut tree was still standing over his body.

We photographed the scene and gathered information about the lay of the general area to assist at the coroner's inquest or inquiry and the body was then taken to the morgue in Nelson. We learned from the other workmen that trees growing on sloping ground like that one would sometimes develop tremendous pressure in the lower end from their constant fight to hold themselves upright. This was obviously one of those trees but why the split had happened in the brief instant that the unfortunate logger was right beside it was purely fate.

Several years after this first incident I was working in the Lardeau River area at the north end of Kootenay Lake. It was a clear calm day in mid-winter and I was checking safety issues on the trucks that were hauling logs to a location where they were bundled and dumped into the lake to be towed to Nelson. There were a few feet of snow on the ground and this was causing a bit of a slowdown in the actual logging in the woods but the trucks and other machines were still very active. My routine was interrupted by a radio call requesting me to go to a logging show only a few miles from where I had been working. The call advised there had been a sudden death as the result of a falling tree.

The location was near the site of the Duncan Dam, which was completed and fully operational by 1967, only a few years after this event. In fact, since construction of the dam began in 1965, it is possible that this logging may have been undertaken to clear the area in preparation for the dam.

At the site I was met by several men who had been working

on the same show as the dead man, a faller who had been relatively new to the job. He was reported to have been a hard worker who hurried the job whenever he could, though there had been no concerns about the safety of his work habits. One of the other workers who had witnessed the accident was the operator of a crawler tractor/bulldozer that had been clearing snow from the serpentine roadway that allowed access to the newly active logging area. This catskinner told me that the faller had struggled through the deep snow to fall the trees on the downhill side of the roadway that he was clearing with his tractor. He had seen the faller working among the trees beside the roadway but he had not seen any trees falling. Then after several passes by the catskinner and his machine, the faller had come to the edge of the road and with hand signals asked him to push over a tree that stood very near the roadway. This was a very simple request so the skinner simply raised his blade to its maximum height and drove his machine up the snowbank until the blade touched the tree that the faller had indicated. The catskinner was amazed at what happened as the indicated tree began to fall; by the time the cloud of snow had cleared, he estimated that ten or twelve trees had fallen in a domino effect from the one he had pushed. The faller had notched and back-cut all of them to accomplish what had just happened, a practice called "gang-falling" that is contrary to many safety regulations in the industry. The faller gave a big smile and a wave as he climbed over the snowbank again to begin bucking, topping and limbing the fallen trees.

    The catskinner went back to clearing and widening the roadway and about half an hour later he again came to the place where the multiple fall had been set up. As he was rolling snow over the bank at the edge of the roadway some of the snow came up against a relatively small tree. Suddenly he realized that this tree was starting to fall into the area where the previous cluster had fallen. Below him he could see the faller standing on one of the downed trees, cutting it into sections. The catskinner revved the engine of his machine and hollered to try and get the faller's attention but he was quite sure of the futility of this due to the noise of the man's chainsaw. The tree struck the faller squarely and killed him instantly.

The stump of the killer tree had been notched and back-cut in the same manner as all the trees that fell in the domino effect. However, in the excitement of the moment of his achievement the faller had failed to see that this one had escaped and it cost him his life. The coroner's inquiry ruled that the faller had died by his own error and the report put some emphasis on the unsafe practice of gang-falling. Though it was contrary to safety regulations, the faller had chosen to gamble on it and lost.

The One That Almost Got Away

In 1967 I transferred to Williams Lake where I was to work Highway Patrol in that detachment area and that of Alexis Creek. Those were the days when hot cars with huge engines were the new toy of choice for the folks who could afford them and on one particularly beautiful summer day when I was working on Highway 97 south of 150-Mile House there were a lot of these folks out and about, all of them in a hell of a hurry. I was using an unmarked patrol car equipped with the new moving radar equipment and I was kept quite busy with speeders of this kind for several hours. Although I should have taken a break to fuel up and get a bite of lunch, traffic work is a little like fishing: if you quit while they are biting, the excitement will be all over when you get back.

I also have to admit to a bad habit of letting the fuel in my car get very low before I refilled. I think I may have developed this trait while running the old tractor on the family farm. After hours and hours of going around and around a field at about four kilometres per hour I never got too far from the fuel source. For those times when the old John Deere did run out of fuel halfway round the field the manufacturer had thoughtfully installed a little back-up tank so that you just flipped a valve and away you went again to complete the round and return to the gasoline cans at the edge of the field. (I know this is a lame excuse for my failure to refill but I'll stick with it!) The problem after I became a police officer was that there were no reserve tanks on police cars and no fuel cans on the shoulder of the highway. This failing of mine was not confined to my working hours. My wife delights in telling about the time we coasted into Cache Creek in our little Volvo in the early darkness of a winter evening. I had anticipated that our fuel supply would take us right into town and even allow for a bit of price checking at the variety of service stations there, but it ran out just as we crested the last hilltop east of the little community. We rolled up to the pumps at the first service station we came to and filled up. And of course, you're right! Gasoline was two cents a gallon cheaper at every other source in town. I could easily have saved twenty cents on the fill-up if our need had not been so urgent.

Now on this particularly beautiful Cariboo summer afternoon as I cruised the highway in my unmarked car, I met a south-bound muscle car standing tall in its suspension as it came over the crown of a hill. It was well inside the effective range of my radar unit and I immediately locked in a reading of ninety-seven miles per hour. Moving radar equipment required the operator to obtain a speed reading from an oncoming vehicle, then stop and turn around to pursue the violator and issue the required paperwork. Most drivers of that era realized what they had done and immediately pulled over and stopped. Many did not!

On this occasion I made clear eye contact with the offending driver as we shot past each other. The whole thing had happened in about one second but I knew instantly from our fleeting eye contact that this guy was not one of those who would pull over and take his medicine. He had nothing to lose by trying to outrun me because if he failed he could reasonably claim that he was just driving fast and had no knowledge of my efforts to overtake him. On the other hand I would have to prove to the court that he had seen me and had deliberately chosen to make a run for it. I braked hard and managed a reverse turn in one smooth sweep and put my foot into the throttle right up to my ankle. The big engine in the two-door Plymouth police car bellowed through the air intake as it accelerated into the pursuit. A glance at the gas gauge told me that I had to take this fellow in a very short time or I would be out of gasoline. I radioed for backup but there was not another police unit between my location and the Trans-Canada Highway at Cache Creek, a distance of 130 kilometres.

As we neared the end of the second mile of the run I caught a glimpse of the runaway driver as he shot past other traffic with very little or no consideration for their safety. At the sound of my siren most of the other drivers braked hard and moved over to allow me through but on a few occasions I was forced to brake heavily and lost time. My fuel gauge was now hard against the little post at the empty mark.

As my runaway approached the hamlet of Lac La Hache there was still about a half mile between us but when I came around the curve into the centre of the village my target was no longer visible, though it should have been if it had stayed on the highway. There was a cloud of dust rising from the right side of the road, however, and I braked and turned into the area where the dust originated. Sliding to a stop behind a roadside service station, I found my target vehicle with its driver just in the act of stepping out of it. He wore a very disappointed expression on his face when he saw me. I immediately jumped out of my car, leaving its big engine chugging and puffing from the extreme exertion it had been through, and told him to stay right where he was. He complied and I was just about to take his driver's licence when my car chugged one last time and went silent.

    I thought of asking the runaway driver to help me push the police car to the fuel pumps but decided against it. Instead, I placed him under arrest for dangerous driving. Meanwhile, one of the service station attendants had come to the back of the garage to see what was unfolding there. He had seen the would-be escapee leave the highway moments before I arrived and now he gleefully told me about it in the presence of the driver. When I told the attendant that I had run out of gasoline, he started laughing so hard I thought he was going to roll on the ground. This display of unbridled mirth did little or nothing for the mindset of my prisoner who was now in the back seat of the police car. Finally the attendant hurried to the front and returned with a can of gas and a funnel. He poured most of the contents into the tank of the police car then carefully drizzled a small portion into the engine's air intake. The big engine roared to life as though nothing had happened and I drove to the pumps at the front of the station and had the man fill 'er up so I could take my client back to the lock-up at Williams Lake. The offender appeared in court the next morning and was on his way again in just over twenty-four hours. Some days are diamonds; some days are stone.

    I have been challenged by many people about the need for and the benefits of speed law enforcement. Most have claimed with some certainty that an alert, high-speed driver in daylight on an open road is not a significant hazard. They may be correct to a certain extent but unfortunately there is no sure way to measure a driver's attention span. On the other hand, almost every experienced policeman has developed a hard-nosed attitude on this topic after attending a few crash sites where a high-speed vehicle has cut another vehicle into pieces and dumped its contents on the road. I have attended several crashes where

The One That Almost Got Away

a speeding vehicle simply left the road and produced a trail of debris and bodies as it spent its kinetic energy over a distance of several hundred metres. One of the stories in my first book tells of a car coming into contact with a moose in the darkness of a winter evening at an approximate speed of 160 kilometres per hour. Seeing the results of such accidents made the issuing of speeding tickets a much easier task for me.

Reality Lost

This incident took place on a beautiful spring day in 1968 when I was working routine highway patrol duty on the central Cariboo Highway not far from Williams Lake. In those days the town was known as the "hub of the Cariboo," a title that came from its place in the Interior forest industry. Logs were trucked there from a one-hundred-mile radius to feed the insatiable appetites of its seven large mills. This involved the services of several hundred logging truck units that were out on the highway all year except during the brief time known as breakup when they were all banned until the frost thawed out of the ground.

On this particular day I was watching for the trucks that were in the habit of turning off the highway onto a very rough and steep piece of road in order to access the mill yards. Its only virtue was that it allowed them to avoid passing over the commercial truck scales where they were frequently ticketed for overloading. Although I was kept quite busy with the constant flow of these trucks and other traffic activity along the highway, on my first pass through an area a few miles north of town I noticed an old fellow sitting in his car at the side of the road. It was well to the side of the travelled portion of the highway so I assumed he was just having a rest and enjoying the nice spring day. I also noticed that his car carried Manitoba registration plates and I wondered what had brought him all that way apparently alone.

    About two hours later I passed this area again and saw that the car and driver were still in the same location. When I pulled in beside the car and spoke to the old fellow it was immediately obvious to me that something was seriously wrong. He had not shaved for at least a week and the odour in the car told me he was in urgent need of personal hygiene but he was unable to tell me where he had been or where he intended to go. The car was littered with wrappers from service station-type food items and drink bottles. After numerous requests and reminders he managed to find his wallet and I obtained his driver's licence, which gave me his name and told me that he was in his late seventies. I radioed this information and his licence plate number to our office and asked for a record search. In those days nearly all routine police bulletins and information were distributed by mail so I was not at all surprised to hear that there was nothing on our files about the man or his car. The address on the driver's licence, however, was in the hometown of one of the policemen in the Williams Lake office, and recalling the man's name from his memories of his hometown, he made a telephone call to his parents.

    The mystery was solved. Everyone in that small prairie community was aware of the missing man and his tragic circumstances and the policeman's parents immediately called his relatives. They were very glad to hear that he had been found and that he was alive because they had feared the worst since his disappearance nine days earlier. The policeman's parents also called their local police office with the information and plans were soon underway to get the missing man back to his home.

TRAGEDY ON JACKASS MOUNTAIN

The old gentleman had been struggling with memory loss for a year or more and his family had become more concerned each day about his safety. They were very reluctant to have him placed in an institution but his behaviour was rapidly deteriorating and they had finally decided that they could no longer cope with the problem on their own resources. On the morning they had chosen to take him to the hospital they woke to find him gone along with his car. To this day I still wonder if the old fellow had "seen the writing on the wall" through the dense fog of his disability, had understood enough to know he was about to be institutionalized and had deliberately run away. Or did he just go for a drive and get lost? Either way he had travelled more than three thousand kilometres before he came to our attention. The fact that he had managed to keep gasoline in his car and obtain the junk-food items that kept him alive would seem to be an indication of the indifference of the many people who must have seen him en route and done nothing to help.

I took the old fellow to the local hospital where the staff cleaned him up and fitted him out with one of their wonderfully fashionable hospital gowns and he was placed in a secure room equipped to prevent him from running away. I visited him later in the day along with the policeman from his hometown and we tried to tell him that one of his sons and his daughter were flying to Williams Lake the next day to take him and his car home. I was unable to be sure if he understood our message but he did seem glad to see us in our uniforms.

He had been a successful Manitoba grain farmer all his life but he and his wife had turned the farming operation over to their children when they retired in the nearby town. They had enjoyed life there for several years before his sudden mental deterioration. Alzheimer's was not commonly known to us at that time but I am now quite certain that he was displaying all of the symptoms of that disease. I heard no more about the old gentleman after that day.

Pinky and the Bad Guys

This story began when a hard-drinking Cariboo couple that I'll call Peter and Polly got themselves a car. The moment one of our detachment's alert street cops saw it and recognized its occupants he radioed the car's description and the licence plate numbers to the office and this bit of information immediately became a local bulletin of interest. The car was just an ordinary standard-sized Chevrolet and would have caused no concern among the local police except for the reputation and continual antics of its new owners. These two had been trouble when they were on foot and we all knew that this vehicle was the start of something really bad.

Peter and Polly were almost continually in court, always the accused subjects in several trials in various stages of adjournment. They were unique in that their criminal activities were not motivated by greed or personal grudges but more by their daring attitude and their complete lack of respect for the safety and rights of everyone around them. They just loved to raise hell and a belly full of liquor put this strange attitude completely in charge of their actions. The most positive thing I can say about them was that they had an aversion to physical violence. In nearly every instance where we dealt with them after one of their foolish stunts they were laughing and jovial about their situation and seemed to think that the nuisance of the police was all part of the fun. Their antics were of such concern to us that one of the first things we did for a newly arrived policeman was to introduce him to Peter and Polly, an introduction that was always a merry occasion with lots of jokes and jibes directed toward us as the fun spoilers.

To this point in time all of their offences had been for a variety of routine nuisance matters but they had all occurred before Peter and Polly had wheels. We were all very aware that their new and greatly increased mobility would lead to a greater abundance of anti-social behaviour. We knew that neither of them would have given any thought to the negative potential of the car; they would only have considered all the fun they were about to have at a much expanded variety of locations.

The car bulletin had only been in circulation for a few days when the vehicle was spotted early one evening parked near their favourite watering hole. A stroll through this establishment by one of our officers determined that Peter and Polly were sitting with their usual select group and both were well on their way to alcohol-induced oblivion. Because of their freshly acquired vehicle, their location and their "three sheets to the wind" status, this news was immediately broadcast on the police radio. Of course, we all knew that if they left the bar and drove away they would be among a fine company of inebriates. In those days, certainly in the Cariboo, well over half of the cars on the street after 1:00 a.m. were driven by drunken or impaired drivers. Peter and Polly would only be different from the rest of this gang because of their attitude.

Now it happened that our local RCMP detachment had recently been blessed with a new constable who had just completed his training at Regina. Newly arrived people, whether brand-new recruits or senior members, were always subjected to close observation by the established members of any detachment, all of them checking to see how the newcomer reacted to each situation. In this case, the new arrival was cause for more than the usual comments and observations by the old-timers because he walked with a ram-rod straight posture and he swung his arms almost as though he was still on the parade square at the training division. He unfailingly wore his issue cap and gloves and it seemed he could not leave the office or his patrol car without subjecting himself to an imaginary kit inspection as he had been subjected to so frequently during training. In all fairness I have to admit that he seemed to be capable and knowledgeable but he was extremely slow in completing even the most routine task and he also seemed totally unable to determine the difference between an emergency event and one that was regular boring routine. It did not take long for one of the senior constables to dub our new member "Pinky" and the new handle stuck like shit on a blanket. The unfortunate fellow accepted it but it did not make him alter his deportment or behaviour.

In those days a new member was moved into the shift-work routine after a very short orientation at his new post. The senior people would help the new guy whenever they were available but our manpower situation generally left him on his own much of the time. This was the situation for our most recent arrival. In a very short time Pinky was assigned a position on the shift-work schedule the same as everyone else, regardless of their level of experience. So it happened that on this memorable evening Pinky was the lone night shift man when the last of the evening shift finished up their paperwork and went home. Peter and Polly were still at their favourite watering hole when the last evening shift worker made his final pass around town. Their car had not moved. This information was passed to Pinky with the suggestion that he keep a watch for the car and be prepared for something out of the ordinary and he no doubt pulled over to the side of the road and made entries on his clipboard about the description of the car and occupants. He then confirmed receipt of the information as he had been taught.

    I had finished my shift before midnight that evening and gone home to bed. However, back in Nelson during my first year on the traffic section I had received training as a breathalyzer operator, a skill that had greatly increased my time in court and also assured that I seldom spent the entire night in bed. As I was also the traffic member on call that night I had the highway patrol car parked at my house. It was about 2:30 in the morning when the telephone rang and I answered to hear Mel, our detachment's night shift prisoner guard, on the line. The prison guard was one of the most important people at rural and small town RCMP offices, his primary function being the care and security of prisoners, but his duties also included answering the telephone and the police radio and dealing with the public at the front counter. A good prisoner guard with a wealth of common sense was the equivalent of having another policeman on the shift and Mel was one of the best. A very long-time resident of the community, he had a wealth of knowledge about nearly every citizen and a wonderful sense of humour, which he knew exactly how and when to apply.

    When I answered my phone on this occasion he told me a rather odd story, which left both of us wondering if we should be laughing or angry. Apparently, around 1:00 a.m. Pinky had discovered Peter and Polly driving around the streets of this rather small community and he began calling their location to the office. He told Mel that they had chosen not to stop in spite of him displaying the emergency equipment on his marked patrol car and had just continued to drive along at a maximum speed of about thirty miles per hour. This performance had gone on for nearly an hour before they finally pulled the car onto the shoulder of the road and stopped. Pinky also stopped the patrol car but about fifty feet to the rear of their car. He placed the car in the park position, set the emergency brake, placed his hat squarely on his head, put on his gloves, called the location of the stop to the office, and finally picked up his clipboard and flashlight from the passenger seat and got out of the car. Just as he had almost completed the walk between the stationary cars, Peter and Polly slowly drove away. Pinky returned to the patrol car. He carefully placed his clipboard, cap, gloves and flashlight on the passenger seat, released the parking brake and shifted the car to drive. He called on the radio to advise Mel what had happened and that the circus was back on the road. Through a lot of laughter Mel told me that this scenario had been repeated four or five times and he thought that I should come out and put a stop to it.

I got into my uniform and was out the door of my house within five minutes. I started the patrol car and called to Pinky as soon as the radio came on. I could hear the excitement in his voice as he gave me their location and direction of travel. I asked him what speed they were travelling and he immediately called back with more excitement in his voice. "Twenty-five!" he shouted. During this exchange I had overtaken the parade and, without turning on my emergency lights, I came up behind Pinky and talked to him by radio. I told him to move alongside the pursued vehicle with his emergency lights on and to crowd them a bit to the right to make it plain that they were now required to stop. As he followed my instructions the car moved to the extreme right and slowed quickly. Pinky braked hard and came to a stop behind the suspect car but I was amazed to see the distance he left between his own car and that of the suspect and even more amazed to see that he was obviously not going to correct this situation.

I immediately passed the two units, pulled in front of the suspect vehicle and quickly backed toward it until there were only inches between the cars. I jumped out and was beside the driver's door before the driver realized that there were now two police cars. Polly was at the wheel and Peter was gesturing wildly from the passenger seat, telling her to back up and go around my patrol car. I tried the door handle but the door was locked and the window tightly closed. As she grasped the gear shift lever in an attempt to back away I put the heel of my boot into the window beside her with all the force I could muster. The window exploded into thousands of little fragments and I instantly had access to the interior of the car. Polly was obviously more than a little shaken by this; her mouth and eyes were wide open but she made no sound. I reached into the car and turned off the engine.

Pinky had been almost completely out of his car when the window exploded and just as I retrieved the ignition key he approached at a brisk walk, swinging his arms. Like Polly, he too was wide-eyed. He came up to the driver's door and looked in through the empty window opening. Then he backed away and immediately walked around to the passenger side of the now immobilized car. On his arrival there he reared back and kicked out the other window. I am not sure just why he did this but I suspect it was to vent some pent-up frustration.

I coached Pinky through the process of arresting Polly for impaired driving and we took the pair to the office. Peter spent the night with us for being drunk in a public place and Polly submitted a breath test, which I administered, and she was then officially charged with impaired driving before we placed her in custody for the remainder of the night.

I was home again and in bed in just under two hours. "That wasn't so bad," I told myself. A routine call just to do a breathalyzer test almost always took that much time. The time involved was of no consequence to the RCMP as overtime pay was still years into the future.

Peter and Polly now had some new items on their pending list of court cases, items that would be dealt with mainly by the passage of time. There was, however, one very positive result from that night of fun and games: Peter and Polly disposed of their now windowless car and they chose not to replace it.

Giants at Alcohol Lake

About fifty-five kilometres to the south and west of Williams Lake there is a Native reserve that is correctly known as Alkali Lake but back in the late sixties those of us in the local RCMP establishment knew it as "Alcohol Lake." This title came about not only from the similarity of the words but also from the reputation that had been earned by many of the residents of this tragic place over many years of despair and neglect. A number of the men from the Alkali Lake reserve were part of the group of Williams Lake street people who were referred to as the "Troopers" both by themselves and by the police. They were a hard-drinking bunch who spent many of their nights in the RCMP cells due to being intoxicated in public places.

However, while we in the police establishment and the general population of Williams Lake were mainly aware of those Native people who frequented the streets and alleys of the town, there was another side to the people of Alkali Lake. The reserve village was adjacent to the headquarters of one of the oldest cattle ranches in the Interior of BC, a ranch that had been established during the Cariboo gold rush by Herman Otto Bowe, who had actually come west as a gold seeker but had seen the potential for a cattle operation in this most beautiful valley. Bowe's original name for the ranch, "Paradise Valley Ranch," was later changed to "Alkali Lake Ranch" and as such became an important part of provincial history. Bowe and a partner, Philip Grinder, both married women from the nearby Native band and for several generations their offspring ran the operation, after which it changed ownership numerous times.

Most of the lands held by this ranch are inaccessible by vehicle so its successful operation has always depended to a large extent on the availability of cowboys from the Alkali Lake reserve and this interdependency brought about a mutual trust and understanding between the ranch owners and the Native people. The workers from the Alkali Lake Ranch and reserve seldom came to town and when they did they had a list of tasks that took up all their time until the businesses closed for the night and they hurried back to their homes to prepare for their work activities of the next day. They never came to the attention of the police, so they were almost invisible to us, and it was only during the annual Williams Lake Rodeo that we saw them.

The rodeo brought nearly all the ranchers and the Natives into the community for this huge celebration of their way of life. In the early years the rodeo had included an event called the Mountain Race in which riders and horses formed up on the rim of the valley above the town. The sound of the starting gun marked the beginning of an all-out race over the mile or more of steep, rocky and tree-covered mountainside toward the finish line in the rodeo corral on the edge of the little town. Over the years most of these events were won by the fearless riders from the Alkali Lake reserve, most of whom worked at the nearby ranch and had honed their horsemanship skills on a daily basis. Unfortunately, many men and horses were injured in the course of these races, finally forcing the rodeo committee to discontinue it.

Also among those less visible but great citizens of the reserve were Andy Chelsea, who was later elected chief, and his wife, Phyllis, who became the leaders of a group that formulated a grand plan to better the lives of their kin at Alkali Lake. In those days the reserve was plagued by bootleggers, both Native and non-Native, who brought liquor onto the reserve for sale. The temptation was too great for some of the residents and they would spend every cent of their resources on liquor, and the following drunken debacles frequently resulted in death or serious injuries. The Chelseas aimed to change all this and they gathered a group of carefully selected women of the reserve and men who worked on the ranch or with the few other employers in the area. Their goal was to have the Alkali Lake reserve declared a "dry reserve," something that was almost unheard of in the late 1960s.

During my time in Williams Lake I met with a few members of the group trying to improve conditions there and I must admit that I looked on their ambitious goal as truly admirable but, in reality, almost impossible to achieve. I believe that this negative attitude was also in the minds of many of the people in the group but they somehow persevered with outward optimism that did not allow their dream plan to die or become dormant. Some of the other members were Irene and Freddie Johnson and Mabel Johnson but the one that I remember most clearly was Margaret Samson because she was not typical of the group. She had spent time in Williams Lake with the hard-drinking street people and at other times of her life she had chosen sobriety. She was constantly at war within herself about the choices that had to be made between the two lifestyles but in the early 1980s she chose sobriety and has maintained that status ever since.

Margaret displays the typical Native sense of humour when she tells people that in the "bad times" she did not just "fall off the wagon," she jumped.

I was transferred out of Williams Lake while the dry plan was still in its infancy and I left still convinced that it would not happen. However, I kept track of the group's progress from my next location and a few years later I was very pleased to read a news account of the proclamation that brought their dream to reality. After this "dry law" was in place, the bootleggers could be, and were, immediately ordered off the reserve.

Early in 1989 I retired from the RCMP and began a second career as a civil servant with the provincial government in the section that looked after the licensing of firearms dealers. After my first five years there, office politics and my unbending attitude took me to the BC Gaming Licensing bureaucracy and one of my duties in this new and mind-numbing situation was the licensing of bingo games throughout the province. In one of the many files that I processed was an application for a bingo licence for the Native community at Alkali Lake. It was signed by Margaret Samson and I immediately called her and we had a great visit. She recalled our meeting all those years earlier and proudly updated me on the dry status of the reserve and how it had been such a positive step for all of the people there. With obvious pride in her voice Margaret told me about the years that she had continued to push and motivate the members of her committee and how they constantly attended political meetings, continuously keeping their goal in the minds of those who could make it happen. The persistence and patience of this determined group were finally rewarded.

Over the years there have been many violations of the band ordinance against liquor and no doubt these problems will continue. The most positive aspect of the band law, however, is that whenever there is a violation, the band authorities have the right and the duty to deal with the perpetrators and this is being done without fail. All the members of this original group of determined people along with Margaret Samson should be remembered for their foresight and grit in bringing about this very necessary improvement to the lives of all the residents of the Alkali Lake reserve.

Corporal Punishment

It was toward the end of the summer of 1969 that my family and I were transferred from Williams Lake to Lytton, a small community at the confluence of the Thompson and Fraser rivers. I was to become the constable in charge of a two-man highway patrol unit there, and although the new position would not result in any additional pay, it would be a step closer to an eventual promotion.

My new unit's services were spread pretty thinly as our patrol district included the Lytton, Lillooet and Spences Bridge detachment areas. Fortunately, Lillooet was not a heavily travelled area so my attendance there was mainly to assist with the investigation of vehicle crashes and perform mechanical safety examinations of school buses and transport trucks (a skill in which I had received additional training during my first year on traffic detail in Nelson). The Trans-Canada Highway, however, ran the full length of both the Lytton and Spences Bridge detachments and as a result this hundred kilometres of roadway plus several hundred kilometres of secondary roads demanded nearly all of our time. In an effort to provide coverage of the whole area, the other constable and I seldom worked together; our shifts were from approximately 8:00 a.m. to 4:30 p.m. and from 4:30 p.m. to 1:00 a.m. We usually took time for a bit of debriefing at the start of the afternoon shift in order to keep up to speed on what was happening out on the road but this debriefing also helped us to ensure that our patrol was seen at least once a day along the entire length of our section of the highway. We were each entitled to one day off every week, usually between Monday and Thursday.

When I received my new posting, my wife and I were told that there was only one rental home in the Lytton community that would be suitable for our family of four so our move there would depend on our ability to make a suitable rental agreement with the property owner. Patricia and I sat down to discuss the options and we quickly found there were very few: if this one and only available home was not suitable for us, the move would not happen. Either of us could have made the call about the house but it was decided that, since a police vehicle was available to make the 570-kilometre round trip, I would drive to Lytton and make the arrangements or decide against it if that seemed the thing to do. In Lytton I met our new landlord and found the home to be quite suitable to our needs. It was situated on a small lot near the centre of the little community with all facilities within walking distance. The owner and I sealed our rental agreement with a handshake and I drove back to Williams Lake the same day. Time accelerated for us and our little family; there was a farewell party and I worked on wrapping up my open files in preparation for the move. In less than thirty days we were on our way.

I still clearly remember our family's arrival in Lytton. The Trans-Canada Highway passes just above the Lytton townsite, which sits on a bench above the Fraser River. An access road loops down from the highway through a Native reserve on the upstream side of the town then through the town itself and back up to the highway at the opposite end. The reserve at Lytton was typical for the BC Interior: a row of rundown houses on each side of the road with a mission church near the middle on one side. Derelict vehicles were present in the front yard of nearly every home; some still had wheels on them but most had been scavenged for such obviously useful parts. Household white appliances were also much sought-after lawn ornaments here.

My wife, who was born and raised in the Ottawa Valley of Ontario, was wide-eyed as we crossed the Canadian Pacific Railway main line and got our first view of the reserve. From this location the bulk of the Lytton townsite was not visible and anticipating what was going through Patricia's mind I immediately pulled over so we could fully appreciate the scene below us. I held my best poker-face and, pointing out the house directly across from the church, I informed her that the landlord had promised to remove the upside-down vehicle and the refrigerator from our front yard but obviously he had been busy with other tasks in preparation for our arrival. Life in Lytton was going to have some bright moments!

Our new home was actually a beautiful little four-level split with two bedrooms and a very large recreation room. Everything that Lytton had to offer was nearby. The town's post office occupied one corner of our lot and the grocery store was right across the street. The Legion bar was one block down the alley and the hotel beer parlour was two blocks down the main street from our corner. The town swimming pool was less than two short blocks away and the elementary school was four blocks away on the border with the Native reserve.

When I had viewed our new home on my initial trip to Lytton, the landlord had been busy cleaning and painting the interior, only stopping long enough to show me around the house and make our handshake rental agreement. Now we found him still cleaning and several of the rooms were lacking their second coat of paint. However, the moving truck had arrived in town along with us and he agreed to let us unload our furniture into the little attached garage. Meanwhile, we took accommodation at the Lytton Pines Motel until the last painting and cleaning was completed to our landlord's satisfaction. This motel living went on for ten days, though it seemed like a month. While the room was of ordinary size and had all the standard fixtures of that era, it was totally inadequate for a busy family of four on a longer than one-day stay, but as it was all there was, we made the best of it. Our oldest child started the first grade within a few days of our arrival and Patricia drove him to school each morning and was there to pick him up at the end of the school day.

The majority of the people in Lytton are Natives whose ancestors have lived in that area for an estimated ten thousand years. Their policing expectations were somewhat different but having been stationed in Williams Lake with its large Native population I knew that dealing with the people of Lytton was not going to provide anything new to me. Native policing was neither more nor less difficult than most other police functions.

On the morning of my first day at my new job I reported to the corporal in charge of the detachment and immediately received a stern lecture. He informed me that my assigned duties on the highway would be secondary to whatever was happening in his detachment. Obviously, I thought, he was trying to be one of the old-school detachment commanders who ruled with an iron fist and little respect for traffic law enforcement officers. I had heard of and seen a good number of his type over my eight years in the force, though there was definitely something more than a little weird about this fellow. I tried to assure him that if there was any kind of an emergency situation, we were all policemen and he could count on the assistance of our highway patrol unit to deal with it. Perhaps I did not use my best judgment when I immediately added that while Lytton was my home base, my patrol area reached into three other detachments and these areas also required and expected our assistance.

He sat like a Buddha, glaring unblinkingly at me for thirty seconds or more, and then he screamed, "So that's the way you want it?"

I left his office after suggesting that we would continue our conversation sometime when he was having a better day.

Several weeks went by during which our corporal avoided me to the point of being rude. Each week he would call a detachment meeting for Thursday afternoon at three. We were all required to attend and at the designated time we would all be sitting around the office while the corporal remained in his little side office with the door closed. For the next ten or fifteen minutes we could hear him pacing and banging desk drawers. The intensity of the noises increased gradually as the minutes ticked away until finally he yanked his door open and barged out in an obvious rage. Then he would rant and curse at all of us through his clenched teeth for not doing our duty to his satisfaction. He never dealt with any specifics, only generalities. After the first of these demonstrations I was quite convinced that the man was mentally unbalanced.

Lytton was generally known as a quiet place from the police point of view and it certainly lived up to its reputation during my first weeks there. Of course, the highway always provided some activity by way of serious vehicle crashes and fatalities but these were routine matters that my unit dealt with from start to finish. Through our regular checking and observation of highway traffic my partner and I also frequently found people in possession of various illicit drugs or stolen property. Meanwhile, the detachment men dealt with the town drunks, thefts, vandalism and whatever other complaints came from the local public. Nothing of a serious nature happened, however, during my first weeks there, though there were a number of minor thefts, mischief and assaults. As a result, for the most part our corporal had very little to do and had he been smart enough to stay out of the way of his men they would have taken care of every incident without his help. He must have imagined some terrible events just waiting to happen, however, and was trying to prepare himself because he seemed to be losing his fragile grip on reality a little more every day.

The last Thursday afternoon meeting before Halloween was even more exciting than previous ones as the corporal was obviously very disturbed by the possibility of the town youths doing something he did not approve of. He found it necessary to rant on and on about what he had heard from some of the local citizens concerning previous Halloweens. The poor fellow seemed ready to explode over something that was still in the future. He ordered all of us to be on foot patrols within the community, an action that would put one policeman on every block in the little town. The corporal took part in this plan, too, donning his long black issue raincoat over his uniform even though the evening was warm and dry. The rest of us had learned that we were better off having nothing to do with this "loose cannon" so he was left to walk the streets and alleys by himself.

We walked around in pairs, dressed in uniform, visiting with the people we encountered along the way. By about midnight the community had settled down and we drifted into the office to remain on standby should further pranks or vandalism happen. Our corporal arrived at the office in a blind rage. He had been hit by thrown eggs at least once in every block that he walked and his black raincoat was slippery from top to bottom with smashed eggs. We learned that he had encountered a local youth whom he suspected of throwing eggs, had pinned the youth against a wall and pointed his service revolver at the boy's head. For some reason the youth and his parents decided not to make an issue of this strange conduct and it passed with very little public notice.

After several more of his screaming demonstrations at the Thursday meetings the rest of us got together to formulate some plan to deal with the problem. We discussed a variety of courses that may or may not have been available to us and finally concluded that we must bring our subdivision or regional office at Kamloops into the equation. On their next day off my partner and one of the guys from the detachment drove to Kamloops and met with the staff sergeant who supervised our part of the region. The two constables outlined the problem and cited several examples of the corporal's strange behaviour. From past experience none of us expected this to solve anything but we would have been wrong to attempt any action without having talked to the next link in the chain of command.

Their report to headquarters in Kamloops resulted in what appeared on the surface to be a routine detachment audit. The staff sergeant came to Lytton, interviewed the corporal at length, looked through the detachment records and then interviewed each of us in the privacy of the corporal's office. During his interviews with the senior constable and me, he discussed his meeting with the corporal. He was mildly concerned by what he had observed but our corporal had put on his best imitation of a sane policeman during the interview. The staff sergeant left after telling us all that he felt things were in reasonably good shape at Lytton and that we could count on the support of his office if the need arose.

I believe that some hint of the two officers' visit to Kamloops must have reached our corporal during the detachment audit because he mellowed somewhat and interfered much less for the next few weeks. Several of the weekly detachment meetings were cancelled and that alone made life much more enjoyable. There was nothing happening that needed discussion at these meetings anyway and we did not need the abuse that was routinely heaped upon us. So life at Lytton was better, though still a bit short of good.

Unfortunately, after a month or six weeks had gone by we could clearly see the situation deteriorating again. Our corporal was again having yelling and screaming fits over things that had no importance and the dreaded detachment meetings were with us once again. I updated the staff sergeant at Kamloops by telephone and he expressed concern but asked that I try to keep the lid on things a little longer. I attempted to talk with the corporal as did the senior constable of the detachment but he could only control himself for a very brief time and then would fly into a rage, bringing the discussions to an end. Now the man's behaviour became the only topic of discussion among us. We were all stressed, not by the nature or volume of our work, but by the sad inabilities of the corporal. In desperation we decided to push the situation to the point where our actions would force a resolution.

At the next detachment meeting we all sat listening to his ranting and abuse until he reached the stage where he addressed each of us directly with a personal attack, complaining about non-specific things but blaming each of us for them. At the end of each of these direct attacks he would pause for a moment and glare at his victim. During the pause after the first direct attack, the targeted constable glared back at him and declared, "This is bullshit!" Our corporal stood frozen in the moment, his face went red and then white as the tension grew.

After what seemed an age, another of the constables broke the silence by saying that he agreed with the "bullshit call" and we all immediately indicated our agreement. This announcement was followed by another period of the corporal's silent rage and then he turned on his heel and went back into his office screaming, "Bullshit!" as he slammed the door. We could hear him pushing furniture around in the closed office but after only a few minutes he opened the door again and we could see that the lower drawer on one side of his office pedestal desk was open. He kicked the drawer shut and the front panel of the drawer fell to the floor as the whole desk recoiled from the force of the kick. "Bullshit!"

he screamed again at the top of his lungs. He bounded out of his office and as he crossed the main office toward the door into his attached quarters he screamed the word again. "Bullshit!" And he disappeared into his quarters with the shotgun-like report of the door slamming behind him.

We were all very concerned about this outburst but at the same time we could not help being more than a little amused. The result of our little "push-back" had far exceeded our expectations. Most of us then went home, leaving the afternoon shift to carry on with their duties, but we advised them to keep a watch for the corporal and to call any or all of us if something unusual occurred. No calls were received and the afternoon shift later reported that all had been quiet around the office building.

At the start of my shift the next morning I attended to paperwork and other routine matters around the office but I began to be concerned when ten o'clock arrived and the corporal had not come in. Earlier I had heard sounds from the attached quarters and I assumed the corporal's two little girls were being prepared for their school day by their mother. I was not looking forward to my next meeting with him but when it seemed it was not about to happen that day I prepared to go out on the highway. As I stepped out of the office I came face to face with the corporal's wife.

The woman was obviously uncomfortable about our meeting and we would not have met except that the door to the police office was right next to the door to the attached quarters where the corporal and his family lived. Except for her smaller than average stature and where our meeting took place I would not have recognized her now even though I had met her on many previous occasions. She could only see from one eye, the other being swollen shut and very discolored, her upper lip was swollen and discolored and there were numerous other bruises and welts on her face and neck. I asked her what had happened. She hesitated for a moment as though she was going to reply but then burst into tears and ran back into her residence. Her appearance left no doubt in my mind that she had suffered a terrible beating and there was also very little room for doubt about who had inflicted this on her.

    I called Vic, the senior constable of the detachment, and asked him to come to the office immediately. I knew that his wife and the corporal's wife had developed a friendship over the months they had been stationed together in Lytton. When he arrived at the office I told him what I had seen. We decided that we would call the corporal into the office side of the building and have the wives get together in the attached quarters in the hope that the beaten woman would confide to her friend and some remedial action could be started.

    By this time, a little more than an hour had passed since I had met the battered wife outside her door. Now I knocked on the common door between the office and the corporal's quarters. The response was very slow but after several rounds of knocking the bleary-eyed corporal answered the door. I told him that we needed him in the office immediately. He began to ask what it was about but he did step into the office and I immediately reached behind him and closed the door and positioned myself so that he could not go back into his residence. I advised him that we were investigating an assault and that he was our suspect. I gave him the standard police warning that "you do not have to say anything and anything you do say may be taken down in writing and used as evidence." Then I asked, "Do you understand the warning?"

    He replied that he did.

    Very shortly after we had invited the corporal into the office, Vic's wife had arrived and gone into the quarters next door. Her husband had briefed her on what to expect there and she had been asked to try to find out if the beaten woman felt that she was still in immediate danger. For the next two hours Vic,

Corporal Punishment

the corporal and I sat in the office, Vic and I conversing quietly in a corner out of hearing of the corporal who sat in his office unmoving and staring out the window. Our suspect smelled strongly of stale liquor and seemed to be in a trance-like state. He obviously did not want to talk to us and we were not disappointed by that decision. While we sat there, three of the other constables arrived and we filled them in on what had taken place. Now we all regretted pushing this tragic individual so far at the meeting the previous afternoon as we were fully aware of how awful the result had been.

After two hours we saw Vic's wife leave the corporal's quarters and walk toward her home. Vic and I entered the corporal's office and shut the door. He remained unmoving and facing the window. I advised him that the other constables would be staying with him and that Vic and I would be away for a short time to try and get to the bottom of what had happened. He was told to remain in the office and that if he attempted to leave he would be subjected to whatever force was necessary to keep him there. At this point the corporal began to question our actions and he became abusive. I shouted him down and said he could use the telephone. If he was not satisfied with that, then we were prepared to use whatever force would be required to secure our position. He immediately quieted down and stayed in his office.

Vic and I headed for his home where his wife told us that the corporal's wife had reluctantly admitted that he had beaten her. He had come home from the office the previous afternoon very upset and over the course of the evening drank a twenty-five-ounce bottle of hard liquor and then became violent toward her. He had beaten her about the head and all over her body until the children were awakened by her screams. When their two little girls appeared, the corporal seemed to come to his senses to some extent and he went to bed where he passed out in a very short time. The beaten wife tried her best to reassure the children and get them back to sleep. She then collapsed on the living room couch where she spent the rest of the night.

We learned that this woman had been raised in a very religious home and felt that she must have been responsible in some way for the beating. She most definitely did not want any intervention by the application of the law or by the internal workings of the RCMP. Her tragic view of this incident must have had its roots in that letter by Paul the Apostle to the Ephesians, Chapter 5 Verses 22 et al., that begins with the words, "Wives, submit yourself unto your own husbands, as unto the Lord. . ." I have to admit that we were simultaneously disappointed and relieved by her position on the matter. We could not help but feel he was getting away with a serious crime but had she chosen to charge the bastard we knew it would have made the national news and every print media in the country.

Vic and I went back to the office where he phoned the corporal's wife. She was very thankful for what we had done but she repeated that she did not wish any further action in any form. She assured Vic that she did not feel she was in immediate danger and asked him to allow her husband to come home. We held a discussion and decided to go along with the wife's wishes then stood close around the corporal while the decision was outlined to him. He began to argue but our presence and our menacing attitude stopped him short. Our parting shot was that if any harm came to his family the consequences for him would be very serious.

We updated the Kamloops office and requested some form of action to relieve the corporal of his duties in Lytton. The staff sergeant who had visited us a short time before advised us that action was already underway to move the corporal back to his previous administrative location a few hundred kilometres away where they hoped he would be better able to cope.

Within a very short time the moving van arrived and the

Corporal Punishment

corporal and his family were whisked back to his old detachment. I had also been stationed at that location at one time and knew many of the members still working there, and I could not help making a phone call to one of them. "Hello Mike. How in hell are you?" I asked. "Tell me, did you guys lose some kind of a contest?" I will spare my readers the blistering adjectives that flowed freely in his reply.

Jackass Mountain— A Hard Climb

Jackass Mountain is not a very obvious landmark in the overall ruggedness of the Fraser Canyon Highway route. Its name goes back to the Cariboo gold rush days when a mule-skinner forced a train of pack animals up the canyon, each carrying a maximum load of goods for the mining camps. As every pound of freight that was conveyed into the goldfields meant money in the pockets of the freighters, there is no doubt that the well-being of the pack animals was not their highest priority. The story goes that one heavily laden mule, having struggled up the steep south slope of the grade, was making its way through the narrow rock cut at the highest point when it suddenly reared up and threw itself and its load over the side to certain death. This was the birth of the legend of Jackass Mountain.

My own Jackass Mountain story begins just before noon on a summer's day when a young man from the Native reserve on the north slope of Jackass Mountain came to the RCMP office in Lytton to tell us that he had been walking along the railway track far below the highway at twilight the previous evening. The canyon wind had subsided and the air had become quite calm when he suddenly became aware of an overpowering stench that seemed to be drifting down from the area between the highway and the railway tracks. The young man was quite sure that there was either a dead person or animal not far above the railway track but he couldn't spot it in the patchy forest cover.

The Lytton office called me by radio to give me the details and a short time later I was parking my patrol car on the summit of the Jackass. Walking along the edge of the highway in the area far above where the odour had been reported, I studied the slope below the highway from every available vantage point until I was able to see what may have been a debris trail from a vehicle crashing down the mountain from somewhere near the summit. I was then able to determine the approximate place where it would have left the highway and used the car radio to call my findings to the Lytton office.

I soon found the scuff marks and the slight shifting of a concrete guardrail where a vehicle had obviously left the travelled portion of the road and vaulted the rail. I could see that it had been northbound and was nearing the end of a long straight uphill section of the road when it had crossed the oncoming lanes and headed for the guardrail but there were no marks to indicate that the driver had braked or swerved prior to launching into space. There was still the possibility of a vehicle collision but unless it had been a hit and run situation there were no marks or debris to support this thesis. I concluded that the driver had simply fallen asleep and driven off the road. The vehicle had scuffed over some rocks just outside the guardrail and after that there was only Fraser Canyon fresh air for the car to pass through for its next forty-five metres of travel to where it would have contacted the steeply piled broken rock of the mountainside.

The only option was to climb down there and try to find it. At that time I carried a device called a portable radio in my patrol car but it was actually only marginally portable as it weighed over four kilograms. Taking it into such an area would only add to the hazards and there was a strong possibility that the signal would not reach out of the narrow confines of the canyon anyway. Instead, I called the Lytton office and told them that I would be out of contact for whatever time it took me to climb down to the car and back. The office advised me that they had found a missing person report about a man from the Fraser Valley who was thought to be on a trip into the BC Interior to visit friends. He had failed to arrive as planned and the family had not heard from him for ten or eleven days. The missing man was reported to be an alcohol abuser, a condition which definitely did not go well with trying to drive the Fraser Canyon.

In those days our standard summer working uniform was a shirt and tie with riding breeches and boots. I kept my boots as polished and clean as possible, which was no small task in the great variety of places that my duties took me. Now, giving a few sad thoughts to what they were about to be exposed to I removed my riding spurs and left them in the police car and then climbed over the guardrail. I had not gone far when I realized that I was going to do severe damage to the finish of my beautiful boots and from that point on the climb became a little easier as I put the boots and their condition out of my mind. At the time of this incident I had been in the police business for about ten years; the recovery of decomposing bodies was no longer a new experience to me. I had briefly considered taking an hour to go home and change into more suitable climbing garb but my sense of duty and my curiosity would not allow that. My poor old boots would just have to take what was coming to them; there was a body down there and perhaps more than one.

As I began the descent I tried to avoid areas of material that could be better described as gravel rather than rock as these deposits were unstable and tended to slide out from under my feet. Large rocks that weighed several hundred kilograms or more were much less likely to shift from my weight on them. A few minutes of scrambling over and around the rocks of the mountainside took me to the first heavy impact area where the vehicle had crashed. It appeared the car had been falling front end first and the front bumper had been the first part to contact the mountainside. I could see that it had hooked into the rocks and the car body had gone end over end, crushing the roof to the level of the seats. This was borne out by the smashed windshield lying nearby, held together only by its inner plastic lamination. Around it were thousands of small glass particles, which had come from the case-hardened side and rear windows of the car.

The crushed windshield also showed dark stains, which may have been dried blood, indicating that the person or persons in the car may have fallen or been thrown out at this first major impact. I made my way farther down the trail of the crashing vehicle to where I could see the crushed and twisted remains of a car where it had come to a stop against a cluster of trees that had somehow managed to survive on that rocky slope. It was another 150 metres below my location but this part of the mountainside was a little less steep than what I had just made my way down and I was able to reach it with less difficulty.

As soon as I reached the wreck, I found the source of the foul odour that the young man had reported to us. The body of a man lay beside the car. It was clothed in working attire—jeans and a long sleeved shirt—and it was a wriggling mass of maggots. A massive head injury was obvious and conclusive evidence that the man had not lived to suffer after the car's initial contact with the mountainside. A search above and below the wreckage showed no signs of any other persons having been in the car with the dead man.

I made my way back to the highway along the same route I had come down and reported back to the Lytton office where arrangements were made for the local search and rescue people to assist with the recovery of the remains. The licence plate numbers I had recorded from the wreck connected it to the missing person report and the family was contacted by the police in their home district. When the search and rescue volunteers arrived I made another climb down to the wreckage with them. We bagged the remains and dragged it back up to the highway on a steel toboggan-like device, which was standard equipment for rescue work in the canyon. A routine autopsy was done on the remains and it confirmed that the cause of death was the massive head injury that I had observed and that the man had been alive at the time of the injury. A blood sample revealed an extremely high blood alcohol level, well into the range that could have caused death in a person without an established tolerance. The only remaining doubt was the possibility that decomposition of the body may have produced additional alcohol in the test sample. (With the vastly improved laboratory procedures of today, this doubt may have been eliminated. DNA and nuclear analysis in modern laboratories may have even been able to detect an elevated mood among the maggots!)

Another day in the life of a Fraser Canyon cop was almost at an end. That night after supper I fetched out my supply of boot polish, brushes and rags. Two hours of brushing and polishing and buffing brought my boots back to almost as good a condition as they had been in when I had answered the Jackass Mountain call earlier that day. The following day I returned to the crash location planning to get some detailed photographs of the shifted guardrail and the highway leading up to the point where the car had left the road. As I neared the Jackass summit from the north, a woman standing beside a car parked on the shoulder began to wave frantically for me to stop. I pulled over and she ran to my

Jackass Mountain—A Hard Climb

car to tell me that she had just seen an oncoming car leave the highway and it had gone out of sight down toward the river. She had been about to meet this car when it turned quite abruptly to the right and simply left the road, going almost squarely over the edge. She had caught a glimpse of the driver and she was quite certain he was a black man.

The lady had immediately pulled off the road to the left and parked near where the car had disappeared. She got out as quickly as she could and looked over the side. The slope the car had gone down was quite steep but there were a number of trees scattered over the area and all of them appeared adequate to have stopped a car if it had come into contact with them. The car, however, had disappeared from sight, leaving only a trail of freshly disturbed rocks and earth as it made its way down to where it plunged over the next shoulder of the mountainside. The slope here was steep but there were no vertical drops along the course the car had taken, and from what I could see it appeared to have remained upright, curving left and right as though it was deliberately avoiding contact with the trees.

I had visited this section of the canyon wall on several previous occasions so I had some knowledge of the lay of the ground down there. From the point where the car had gone out of sight I knew there were far fewer trees and the slope became just a bit steeper. This open slope went on for about a hundred metres more and then became an almost vertical drop of several hundred metres to the railway tracks. I called the Lytton office immediately to ask them to advise the Canadian National Railway that there may be an occupied vehicle on their main line below Jackass Mountain. I thanked the witness for reporting the matter, recorded her name and address and advised her she was free to go if she wished to do so.

I took the spurs off my freshly polished riding boots as I said to myself, "My goodness, this is getting to be a regular occurrence."

(Or words to that effect!) I advised the Lytton office that I would again be out of the car doing some mountain climbing and away I went over the steeply piled broken rock. I made fairly good time until I reached the shoulder where the track had gone out of sight from my highway location. From that point I was able to see over the more open mountainside to where the trail of disturbed ground disappeared again over the edge of what I was quite certain was the near vertical drop to the railway tracks. At about the mid-point of this open slope I could see a man sitting on a rock. I called to him and he looked up the slope to where I was standing. He shouted back to tell me he was hurt but he didn't think he had any broken bones or serious injuries. I suggested he should stay where he was and I made my way down, being careful to stay out of the line directly above him so that any rocks I loosened would not fall near or on him. When I reached him, the man told me he was a member of the United States military and he was transferring from a base in Alaska to the Seattle area. He had been rushing the trip far too much and became exhausted and sleep-deprived, and although he remembered a few landmarks he had passed earlier, the last part of the road he had just travelled was just a blur in his memory.

He had been awakened very abruptly as the front of his car dropped over the edge of the roadway but by then there was nothing he could do to stop the plunge. He stood on the brakes, at the same time trying to steer into one of the scattered trees but they continued to pass him on either side as the rather low-speed fall continued. Then suddenly he realized that the mountainside had become much steeper and there were no more trees. The car was now increasing in speed so he decided to bail out. Throwing open his door, he rolled out onto the rocks. He stopped very quickly but his car and all his possessions continued down the hill and disappeared over the next pitch of the mountainside. He had some rather serious abrasions from his intimate contact with the rocks but had he stayed with the car it would have meant certain death.

About the time I had sighted the man on the rock I heard the sound of a train coming down the canyon, and now I was very relieved to hear the throttles closing along with the sound of braking. When the locomotives were directly below our location though still not within our field of vision, the train slowed to a near stop. I had already explained to the man about the rail line just below us and that I suspected the remains of his car were on or very near the tracks. Now he listened very wide-eyed to the sounds of the train and he too looked very relieved to hear the sounds of braking.

The next thing we heard was the throttles being opened again and the train carried on down the canyon. I tried to assure the man that this indicated that his car must be clear of the rails, which would make it easier to recover the wreckage and its contents. Slowly the two of us made our way up to the highway where we learned by radio that the train crew had seen the car and that it was well clear of the rails. I took the man to the little hospital in Lytton where his cuts and scrapes were cleaned and dressings applied as necessary. He was released within a few hours.

There happened to be a work train in the canyon near the location of the car and arrangements were made to have it loaded onto a flat car and moved onto a siding in Lytton. Amazingly, although that vehicle would never return to the road again, it had hung together very well and all the man's possessions were still in it and in fairly good condition. While he had experienced a bit of tough luck when he left the road, from that point on his guardian angel had intervened in a big way. He was on his way again the next day and probably only a little late arriving at his new post.

As for me, I spent the second evening in a row working on my riding boots and after a couple of hours they again looked quite serviceable. All part of a day's work for a day's pay.

Bad Luck on Jackass Mountain

Late one Friday evening three vehicles approached the summit of Jackass Mountain on the Trans-Canada Highway just south of Lytton. Two were standard-sized passenger cars travelling in opposite directions, each with a lone male driver; the third was a full-sized pickup truck with two men in the cab. The car headed toward Vancouver was driven by a man who worked for the provincial government. Normally he lived and worked in the Vancouver area but he had been on a temporary assignment in the Interior. He had been late completing his work but, being a dedicated worker, had chosen to finish rather than return the following week.

The car headed toward the Interior was driven by a man who had been on a business trip to Vancouver. He had completed his business about mid-afternoon but had then joined some associates at a drinking establishment. Therefore, as he drove home he was fighting the dual effects of alcohol and fatigue.

Approaching the summit of Jackass Mountain, he was nearing the end of the long straight uphill climb where the road bends to the left and enters the winding part over the highest section of the road. It was at this point that he lost his concentration or dozed momentarily and the right wheels of his car dropped off the edge of the pavement. He reacted by yanking the steering wheel hard to the left, which resulted in his car lurching across the highway into a head-on collision with the Vancouver-bound vehicle. As there was a concrete guardrail along the edge of the travelled portion the Vancouver-bound driver could do nothing except lock his brakes. Fortunately, both vehicles were travelling under the speed limit, most likely due to the warning signs along this winding part of the highway, and the force of the impact resulted in severe damage to both vehicles but neither of the drivers was badly hurt.

For a moment after the impact, these two drivers remained sitting in their damaged cars and it was at this point that the two men in the full-sized pickup truck heading toward Vancouver came upon the scene. These two were well beyond alcohol impairment. They were drunk. They carried a supply of liquor in their truck and both had been drinking as they travelled. Even if the driver of the truck had seen the crashed cars in front of him, there was no time for his alcohol-fuddled brain to process the information before he ploughed into them. The car driven by the Vancouver-bound man was sandwiched between the truck and the other car, with the roof of his car humped upward by the force of the truck striking the rear end. The impact caused the passenger in the truck to stick his head and face into the windshield with such force that he left a head-sized bulge in the pliable material of the smashed window. The truck's steering wheel was twisted and bent by the force of the driver's weight against it.

At the Lytton RCMP office a call came advising that there was a three-vehicle collision on the top of Jackass Mountain and that there were serious injuries. We arrived at the scene before the volunteer ambulance crew got there. The two drunks were still in the cab of the truck and the impaired driver was still in the Interior-bound car. The driver from the car that had been headed toward Vancouver was nowhere to be found.

The drunks in the truck were useless to us in our attempt to find out what had happened. They thought someone had tried to talk to them right after the crash but both were so incoherent we could only guess what they were trying to say. The driver of the other car told us that he had talked to a man whom he believed was the driver of the car he had hit. The man had asked him if he was hurt, and when he had replied that he thought he was only bruised and shocked, the man had suggested that he should stay in his car until help arrived. The car driver stated that the mystery person had approached his car from the driver's side and that he had been standing outside the concrete guardrail, which was tight against the side of his car after the second impact.

A transport truck had been the next vehicle to arrive on the scene and it came from behind the drunks in the pickup. The trucker was obviously very alert because he was able to stop short of hitting the crashed vehicles. He immediately ran back past the rear of his unit and put incendiary flares on the highway in the hope of preventing other traffic from piling into the accident scene. These flares were still very visible and doing their job when we arrived on the scene. The trucker told us that he was not sure how long before he arrived that the accident had occurred but felt it had been only a matter of minutes. He could not recall seeing the driver of the middle vehicle and he was quite sure there had been no one on foot around the accident scene when he arrived, though he admitted that he had been entirely occupied with getting his machine stopped before he, too, crashed into it so it was possible he might have been mistaken.

The ambulance arrived and we loaded the drunk who had

bitten into the windshield. He had a broken jaw and cheek bones and lacerations all over his head. I took temporary custody of the other two and conducted breath tests. It was obvious to me before I administered the tests that one was drunk and the other impaired and I was proved right: the pickup truck driver showed a blood alcohol level of two hundred and sixty milligrams of alcohol in one hundred millilitres of blood and the other driver had one hundred milligrams of alcohol in one hundred millilitres of blood. I then took these two to the hospital where they were treated for cracked ribs and bruises and then released.

I returned to the crash scene to find that my partners had photographed, marked and measured the scene and that the last of the wreckage was about to be removed. They had also contacted the CBC radio centre that operated the small satellite radio stations along the Trans-Canada Highway in our area and the station had made several appeals asking any motorist who may have picked up a man near the accident scene to contact the police with any information they may have about his whereabouts. Meanwhile, the police members who were working at the scene had searched the entire area in case the driver had walked away and then blacked out or died from his injuries. We then attempted to search the extremely steep mountainside above and below the accident location, but as the lighting equipment available to us was very limited and the extent of our search area was purely speculation, we found nothing.

After several hours the crash site was finally cleared and normal traffic flow was restored. We all went home for a few hours of sleep but at the first traces of daylight we were back in the area. The section of the highway where these vehicles had crashed had a concrete guardrail along the outside of the highway and that portion of it beside the crash site was of the type that is pre-cast in sections and then hooked together end to end. There was solid ground outside this guardrail and the impaired driver had told us that the man who had talked to him had walked along outside the guardrail to approach his car.

However, this pre-cast rail only ran alongside the roadway toward the summit for about sixty metres and there it met a poured concrete retaining wall that created the support for the two-lane highway over the top of the mountain. Where this poured wall met the pre-cast guardrail its outside height was about six metres but the mountainside quickly dropped away so that a little farther along the wall was nearly thirty metres high and almost vertical. From the surface of the highway and in the dark that poured retaining wall looked quite similar in appearance and height to the pre-cast guardrail at the crash site and it was on the rocks at the foot of the high retaining wall that we found the body of the missing driver along with a smashed hand-held flashlight.

We speculated that the Vancouver-bound driver had checked on the condition of the others in the crash and then decided to walk to the curve near the mountaintop to warn other traffic. He had probably walked or run along the edge of the highway inside the guardrail in an attempt to get to the place where he could warn approaching traffic. He then saw the lights of an approaching vehicle—no doubt those of the transport truck that was the first onto the scene—so the man then stepped over what he assumed was a continuation of the pre-cast concrete guardrail. While there had been solid ground outside the rail alongside the crash site, there was nothing but air for nearly thirty metres at the spot where he stepped over. The injuries recorded during the autopsy indicated that he died on impact.

Over the following months we often discussed this incident. It seemed to us that this man had been chosen by the Grim Reaper. He had driven along completely oblivious to this fact until the first car was hurled into his path but he survived. Then before he could begin to react to that first impact, the drunks in the pickup truck had crashed into him but he survived again. Now the Grim Reaper must have been more than a little bent about this mortal. Is he trying to make a fool of me? Let's see you survive this!

The Fraser Canyon, Jackass Mountain and impaired drivers had taken another life. However, the canyon and the mountain are only a little less caring than those who constantly drive under the influence of liquor. We may wish and hope that slogans, posters, advertisements and twenty-four-hour suspensions will be effective but they will never have the necessary effect. Only harsh and unrelenting prosecution will eventually change this situation. I am reminded of an old gem of wisdom that my father quoted occasionally: "If you wish in one hand and then shit in the other, it is very easy to determine which hand holds more."

The Second Man

I was involved in rural policing in the BC Interior for almost all of my years of service with the RCMP. Throughout that period (1962–1989) many of the province's rural areas were very sparsely populated and the policing budget was only a small percentage of what it is today. This combination of circumstances, along with the unavoidable need for occasional police coverage in even the most remote places, necessitated the "one-man detachment" in a surprising number of small settlements.

A "one-man detachment" is not the same thing as today's "one-man policing," which simply means a police person working alone. The one-man detachment of my day was a single police officer working alone within a very large and isolated area with no chance of backup because the nearest person in a police uniform may have been almost two hundred kilometres away on the other side of a snow-clogged mountain pass or an expanse of tidal water. If something went wrong for the officer in such a place— perhaps a serious assault or a firearms or knife attack—backup was out of the question unless some of the local citizens took it upon themselves to help him out. There are, in fact, many stories of how citizens in isolated places came to the aid of their one and only law enforcement officer whenever the need arose.

When BC was still policed by the British Columbia Provincial Police, the province had more than twenty of these one-man police units and most of them remained unchanged for many years after the provincial contract was taken over by the RCMP in 1950. In fact, when I arrived in Nelson as a newly trained RCMP member in 1962 there were still seven one-man units in the Kootenay region alone. I recall talking with several of the men who occupied these locations and hearing how grateful they were that the police radio system had finally improved to the point that they were able to use their car radios from an expanded number of locations in their patrol areas to contact their home offices.

It was, in fact, after the first married policeman began his service in one of those out-of-the-way places that the powers-that-be discovered that they had accidentally acquired extra free policing services for the area. This came about because in those days it was more generally accepted that a wife's place was in the home. As a consequence, in a remote post she automatically became an integral part of the overall police service. The police buildings in most of these one-man detachments consisted of an office with attached living quarters for the officer and his family. The doors to the office and the living quarters were adjacent so the local citizens quickly learned that if the office was not occupied they could simply pound on the other door and tell their problems to the cop's wife. Thus, the wives at these locations automatically became the second "man." They soon learned how to complete an incident report and with only a little more experience they also learned how to settle many of the routine matters that were reported to the local police. I know of many incidents where these women ventured out into the community in the absence of their husbands to take possession of alleged stolen goods or to instruct suspects to leave a disputed item with some neutral party until the officer was available to sort it all out. There were even times when some of these ladies ventured alone into circumstances where a modern-day police officer would be calling for a backup unit. I am quite confident that this co-opting of the wife's services was never made part of the written policy in any police service manual but it was just so abundantly obvious that this was happening that there was no need to commit it to writing.

When I transferred to Lytton in 1969 the Spences Bridge detachment was officially a one-man unit and in January 1971 regimental number 23704 Constable Donald J. Pearson was transferred there from Merritt, BC, where he and his wife Joan had been stationed for three years. Don and Joan had been newly married when they arrived in Merritt but when they moved to Spences Bridge they brought along a new third member of the Pearson family. Little David was very mobile by the time of their move, busy exploring his world and learning to talk, and his mom had her work cut out for her just looking after the household and riding herd on this little whirlwind. However, Joan and Don fell willingly into the police routine at their new location, becoming part of the little community in a very short time. To this day they still have friends there whom they visit whenever possible.

On one of my routine visits to the Spences Bridge detachment that spring I was introduced to two children from the local Native reserve who had been abandoned by their parents. The little boy was close in age to David and his sister was a bottle-fed baby in diapers. The plight of the children had been brought to police attention on a Saturday morning when there had been no other emergency services available so Joan and Don had brought them home with them. It wasn't until the following Monday afternoon that a social worker had arrived to attend to this emergency and by that time these two little additions to the Pearson family were quite comfortable in their new surroundings. Don had located the missing parents and they were in no condition to take care of their children, though his previous experience had taught him that they would be returned to their wayward parents in a very short time. In the meantime, however, the Pearsons knew that a move to yet another temporary placement would be quite traumatic for the little ones so obviously there was only one course of action available: these little people would stay with the Pearson family.

It was around this same time that one of the residents of the village had observed a beautiful Doberman pinscher wandering near the highway. The man approached the dog and found it to be intelligent and gentle. There was no identification on it and it certainly did not belong to anyone in the little community so he decided that it had been either lost or abandoned by someone passing through on the highway. The nearest facility where such an animal could be cared for was more than a hundred kilometres away so the dog also found refuge with the Pearsons. It immediately established its place in the household by showing its great affection and protective instincts for the three children, as well as its respect and admiration for Joan and Don.

Late morning of the first day with the new dog brought another traumatic incident: a head-on crash of two vehicles on the canyon section of the highway toward Lytton. One or more persons were dead, there were severe injuries and traffic flow had been cut off. When the first reports of the incident came to the detachment at Spences Bridge, Don called for emergency assistance from Ashcroft and Lytton and then sped to the scene, leaving Joan in the office/residence to look after the radio, the telephone, the office front counter, their son David, the two little Native children and the new dog. This would be no problem for Joan; after all, she had lived there for several months by that time.

Don arrived at the crash scene to begin recording the

available evidence then quickly discovered that the crash scene was in one of the canyon's radio blind spots. In order to contact his office he had to drive to a nearby hilltop where the radio would function then drive back to the crash site where his radio was again dead. Meanwhile, as the emergency workers' first priority was getting medical assistance for the injured and loading them into ambulances, traffic began piling up on both sides of the site. Finally workers from the Department of Highways managed to restore the flow to one lane but before allowing the cars to move again they talked to the people in those closest to the accident, asking if they had seen the actual crash or anything leading up to it. All those who had seen anything were asked to carry on with their travels but to contact the police at their first opportunity.

As a result, a short time later a line-up began to form at the front counter of the Spences Bridge detachment. They were met by Joan Pearson, who was carefully dividing her attention between the folks at the counter and her other office responsibilities while minding the kids and a dog. I am sure that under better circumstances Joan would have taken statements from the witnesses but in this situation she decided to just record their names, addresses and telephone numbers and a brief note about what they had seen or done.

Now we must remember that this was very shortly after the new dog had arrived on the scene, and David, being a very bright and curious little fellow, and his new friend, the Doberman, were both drawn to the area near the front counter to see the people gathered there; neither of them knew what this was all about but they were certainly going to try and find out. Joan was busily recording information from the last crash witness when she noticed a very obvious bug-eyed expression on that gentleman's face. On following his gaze she immediately saw that little David's attention had been drawn to the obvious dark spot just below the docked tail of the Doberman. Now she could see that the child's finger was up to the knuckle in the big dog's ass. She reached around, plucked the errant finger from its goal and then finished recording the information from the gentleman who immediately left the office, no doubt with an unusual story to tell his friends. A generous application of soap and water resolved this latest problem and everything was once again "good to go." Another routine day for the "second man" was nearing its end.

Police operations today most often see two-person patrols and two units attending if there is even a hint of something a little out of the ordinary. Such was the case at the Vancouver Airport in October 2007 where a confused man who spoke no English lost his life at the hands of four trained police officers. It is very easy to sit in judgment on an incident after the cards have all been dealt and played but I am from the old school and I cannot help but wonder what would have resulted if there had been only one of these four police officers available and he had been duty bound to attend and deal with it. I know from experience that in bygone days the attending officer would have been extremely diplomatic and very resourceful. There is also a strong possibility he would have walked out of the airport along with that unhappy man as they both sought solutions for his problems.

Transport versus Greyhound

From Kamloops going west, the Trans-Canada Highway, the Canadian Pacific and the Canadian National railroads all follow the Thompson River to where it joins the Fraser River at Lytton. The first 112 kilometres of that route pass through generally open country where engineers had plenty of choices for locating the railways and highway, the exception being the area around Kamloops Lake where they were forced to route the Trans-Canada high above the valley floor. Near the hamlet of Spences Bridge, the Thompson canyon narrows and the flow of the river quickens as it struggles through the narrow passage. Here the railways and the highway lie close to each other and very near the river. The only visible sky is almost directly overhead.

Back in the late sixties transport trucks were able to make good time in both directions in the Kamloops to Spences Bridge section of the highway with their speed only restricted as they passed through the town of Cache Creek. The road between

Transport versus Greyhound

Spences Bridge and Hope was a very different matter; it had steep grades and sharp curves that required reduced speed and much greater driver diligence.

The transport truck involved in this story was heading for the coast with a high-volume, enclosed trailer loaded with cardboard boxes that were filled with empty wine bottles. These boxes, stacked on pallets to speed the loading and off-loading process, filled the trailer to the roof, though the total weight was still well short of the maximum that the truck and tractor could legally carry. The unusual thing about a load of this kind was that the trailer became quite top-heavy.

The driver with his load of bottles had passed through Cache Creek and was nearing the end of the open road and easy driving. In those days truckers were paid by the mile, a fact that made it easy to understand why they did not wish to spend any more time than absolutely necessary on each mile. This one had been pushing his truck fairly hard, though it is unlikely that he would have been ticketed for speeding if he had come to the attention of our highway patrol. Our tolerance for speeding vehicles was somewhat more generous in that easier stretch of the highway than in the more confined and winding areas of the canyon just ahead.

About sixteen kilometres north and east of Spences Bridge the highway drops down a steep hill, locally known as the Oregon Jack Hill, and enters a hard right bend as it comes alongside the river and the Canadian Pacific Railway line. Both hill and curve were marked with cautionary signs suggesting a maximum speed of fifty-five kilometres per hour but this driver seems to have been lulled into a dangerous attitude by the relatively easy road he had encountered over the previous 160 kilometres. His truck's tachometer card would later show that he entered the curve at a speed of eighty-five kilometres per hour. However, both truck and trailer could most likely have negotiated that curve at this higher speed with that much weight on board except for the unusual top-heavy nature of the load, and as the trucker fought to stay on his side of the centre line, the trailer began to roll to the outside of the curve, its right wheels leaving the road surface as it started to roll.

Unfortunately, just as this unit came hurtling into the curve, a Greyhound bus was entering the curve from the opposite end. The bus driver saw that the truck and trailer were about to roll but there was no place for him to go. The right edge of the highway was bordered by an almost one-metre-high poured concrete guardrail and retaining wall and beyond it was a fifteen-metre drop to the railway tracks. The bus driver did the only thing he could do: he braked hard and moved the bus as far to the right as possible.

By this time the trailer was nearing a forty-five-degree lean into a rollover and its upper side came into contact with the bus, the impact crushing the upper left front portion of the bus and instantly killing an elderly man seated in the front row above and behind the driver. By far the most seriously injured of the survivors was the bus driver; he suffered a very heavy blow to the head, which resulted in swelling that immediately closed one eye, but he remained conscious and was able to aid and comfort his passengers until emergency services arrived.

The first truly bizarre thing about this whole event was that the impact knocked the trailer back down onto its wheels and the driver continued on as though nothing had happened. A man in a car that had been following the truck witnessed the incident and could hardly believe what he had seen but when the truck continued on its way he began pursuing it, passing it a short distance from the crash site and flagging the driver down. This truck driver, however, had more crust than a pie factory. He climbed down from his rig and claimed that he was not aware of any collision. The man who flagged him down told us later that he had been following the truck into the curve so he could verify that he was going about eighty kilometres per hour. He also told us that he heard the explosive impact and actually felt a shock wave hit his car. This witness had no experience with the trucking industry but he was fully prepared to testify that the driver of this unit could not possibly have been unaware that he had hit the bus because he had to struggle to correct the swaying action of his entire unit after it hit.

We attended the scene from Lytton to assist the lone policeman from Spences Bridge. The ambulance had already attended from Ashcroft and had taken the bus driver and two of his passengers to the hospital there. The elderly man was declared dead by a doctor who happened along shortly after the crash and the dead body was picked up by a vehicle from one of the funeral homes in Kamloops. We photographed, measured and marked the scene before the damaged truck and bus were cleared from the roadway. At the crash site we found a thin black tire mark from the left wheels of the truck trailer and followed it as it crossed the centre line of the highway to the contact point with the bus, which was about one metre left of the double solid line. There was a slight change in the arc of the tire marks at the point of impact and then the mark abruptly ended. We also noted that the damage to the trailer began high and toward the rear on its left side.

There were some interesting conversations around our offices about which charges would be appropriate in this circumstance. The driver had been speeding, he failed to heed the warning signs and he did not react correctly to what he could clearly see ahead of him in broad daylight. He had further complicated his situation by trying to run away from the scene. We settled on a charge of criminal negligence causing death with secondary or backup charges of dangerous driving and leaving the scene of an accident.

About a week after the crash the charges were sworn, the driver notified and his first court appearance in Ashcroft was arranged for a date a few weeks later. Very shortly after the charges were laid, I received a telephone call from a Calgary lawyer who advised that he was representing the trucking company and the accused driver. He continued the conversation with a bit of small talk about the trucking industry and the great cooperation between the police and truckers in general but by that point in my years of RCMP service I had listened to enough of these openings that I knew there was more on his mind. It came with a splash. As soon as he had confirmed that I had attended the crash scene and had a hand in determining the charges he began to unload a stream of abuse on me and all of the police officers who had anything to do with the case. He told me there was not a shred of evidence to support the charge we had chosen and that we would be laughed out of court. He had been in contact with all of the senior drivers from the company and they all insisted that the truck and load could take the crash curve at a far greater speed than eighty-five kilometres per hour. I thanked the lawyer for his call and his kind warning and suggested that I would be prepared for whatever took place in court. I am still not sure what motivated his telephone call but I suspect that the driver and/or the company owner were sitting in his office while he spoke to me.

The first court appearance date came and the matter was set over for a preliminary hearing a few months into the future. I was not in court for that first appearance but I later learned that there had been a great deal of conversation outside the hearing with the trucking company insisting that the unit in question could not have lost control due only to the speed it was travelling. They insisted that there must have been some other unknown factor contributing to the crash.

At that time the court system in BC was still struggling

with trying to be somewhat efficient. To that end, all RCMP detachments of any size had a member on full-time court liaison duty, looking after much of the scheduling of trials and hearings and issuing summonses and subpoenas to bring all matters to the court as soon as possible. In the case of the wayward transport truck a great deal of behind-the-scenes discussion obviously occurred between the defence lawyer and the crown prosecutor and these discussions led to the devising of an almost unbelievable event: a re-enactment at the crash site using an identical truck, trailer and load. This experiment was hardly set up using the scientific method but it was all arranged without any input from the police. The day chosen for the test arrived and a well-known lawyer from the crown office contacted the police to request that they close the highway briefly. Two police units from Ashcroft and Spences Bridge attended and blocked the highway about one and a half kilometres on each side of the original accident scene. The crown prosecutor, a lay magistrate/coroner from Ashcroft and other interested parties who wished to witness the event stationed themselves at the crash site. A company truck that was said to be identical in make, model, structure and load and driven by another very experienced company driver started its test run. Down the Oregon Jack Hill it came, travelling as close as possible to the exact speed that the original transport truck had been going.

 Then just as the truck came into view around that sharp curve, the prosecutor and his friend, the magistrate, took one quick look and started to run. The sight of these runners left an indelible image in the minds of the policemen who were standing a considerably greater distance away. The prosecutor was a much taller than average man and appeared to be on the verge of a new land speed record. The lay magistrate/coroner was of average height but extremely obese and the observers were positive that the man had taken three full strides before the entire mass of his body was underway. The pair were running with tremendous incentive because they both thought they were about to die—and with good reason. The truck and load came around the curve exactly as the previous one had done but this time there was no bus there to knock it back onto its wheels. And had a bus been there to correct the trajectory of the truck and trailer it would probably have killed the two running men on the highway.

The rear end of the truck trailer swung to the outside of the curve and completed its rollover as it came to the edge of the road and the drop-off to the railway track. The rear end and roof of the trailer burst open as it crashed onto its side over the solid concrete retaining wall at the edge of the highway. Bottles flew out of the openings in the trailer and fell to the railway and beyond. I suspect there are still traces of crushed glass there today. The truck tractor came to a stop still attached to the doomed trailer but it had suffered an almost ninety-degree twist in its frame. The driver was uninjured—except for his pride.

We at the police offices were more than a little amused by the result of the experiment. Our glee, however, came mainly from the fact that it was extremely embarrassing to the attending defence lawyer. In our minds the matter could only have been more satisfying if he had been required to clean up the crushed glass and other debris with a dust pan and whisk broom. The experiment's dismal outcome did result in his change of heart and when the preliminary hearing date arrived the original driver pleaded guilty to the lesser charge of dangerous driving. He was fined and given a short suspension of his driver's licence. I have no knowledge of the civil court actions that followed this event but people were a whole lot less inclined to sue in those days. With the excessive number of lawyers among us today there is little doubt that millions of dollars would be won and lost by the participants in such an event; the only true winners being the members of the bar.

Afterwards, the corner at the bottom of Oregon Jack Hill was unofficially named after the transport company that had been involved and in the years that followed this incident truckers came to use that location as a landmark. They all knew exactly where the crash had occurred—and why.

Cold Little Feet

In the summer Lytton is often the hottest spot in Canada with afternoon shade temperatures regularly hitting the mid- to high 30s centigrade and sometimes topping 40°C. In fact, it shares the honour with the nearby town of Lillooet of having enjoyed the second-highest temperature ever recorded in this country: on July 16, 1941, the mercury reached 44.4°C (111.9°F) in both communities. It can also become very cold there and at some point in each of the winters that we lived in Lytton the north wind would push down the canyon and bring some very severe northern Interior weather.

One year just a few days before Christmas, when we were in the midst of one of these icy spells, we received a report at the RCMP office that some children were in distress at an address on the Native reserve at the edge of town. The home in question was very well known to all of us at the police office so two of us attended the call. Although about a foot of snow had fallen at the beginning of this cold snap, the sky was now clear and the sun

Cold Little Feet

was shining brightly but the daytime high was still well below the freezing point. The little house was set back about fifteen metres from the road and the door stood wide open. The path from the road to the door had not been cleared since the recent snowfall but a pathway had been tramped through the snow by tiny bare feet. Inside the house we found the owner of those little feet. A boy about three years old had obviously been home alone with his little sister for a long time. The little girl, who was too young to walk, was sitting on a plastic mattress in a crib. She wore nothing but a little nightgown and a severely overloaded paper diaper. There was no functioning heat source in the home; the oil-burning space heater in the middle of the living room had run out of fuel. The only food visible in the house was a rock-hard, plastic-wrapped, frozen turkey lying on the kitchen table.

The little hero of this story had obviously decided that they were in desperate need of help and he had been running back and forth from the house to the edge of the road until he had polished the full length of the icy path with the warmth of his bare feet. His persistence had paid off because their plight had finally come to the attention of the person who called us.

We scooped up the two little victims and rushed them to the local hospital where they were treated for hypothermia. Fortunately, the human infant is actually pretty tough and these two were a living testimony to that fact. Neither of them had any permanent injuries except for some minor frostbite on the little guy's feet. Immediately on arrival at the hospital they both gulped down nourishment and in a very short time they were soundly asleep in warm beds.

Our next stop was at the local bar where we knew we would find the children's mother, a part-time single mom who was at that time on her own again. She was three sheets to the wind and going for more. We arrested her, placed her in our cells to sober up then reported the matter to the local welfare worker who took temporary custody of the children. Over the following months the mother appeared in court to face charges of endangering children, and following a plea of guilty, she was ordered to pay a token fine. The children were back in her care and custody before spring.

    In the course of my long years of policing and encountering events such as this one I developed a cynical attitude and although I have tried looking back on some of the events with political correctness and rose-coloured glasses, neither of these modern corrective measures have made the memories and the visions any easier to deal with. The memories are still with me and probably always will be and they are made worse by the fact that I know such terrible things are still occurring today. Change is a difficult process and it is always resisted by those who are affected by it.

Kids and Trains

One summer morning I had been delayed in the office by an abundance of paperwork so it was nearly time for my coffee break when I finally cleared the backlog and was ready to hit the highway. One of the detachment guys also happened to be in the office that morning so we decided to take our break together and we jumped into my patrol car to head for a little coffee shop alongside the highway and just above the community. Our route would take us past the Lytton hospital, through the Native reserve and then onto the highway, but as we drove past the hospital we saw a sight that shook us to the core.

A man was running up the outside ramp that led to the second floor of the old structure. This ramp had been added to the building so that stretchers and other wheeled equipment could access the second floor where the little operating room was located. The ramp ran parallel to the street we were driving on so we had a very clear vision of the man and his grizzly bundle. Then before this first man reached the middle of the ramp another appeared at the bottom with a similar burden; he was followed closely by a third man with a tragically similar load in his arms.

Each of the running men was carrying a small child in his arms and we could see the stumps from missing portions of their tiny arms and legs. We knew immediately that the children had come into contact with the wheels of a train. I parked the car and we followed the procession into the hospital where we learned from one of the men that these preschoolers had been on the Canadian National Railway bridge, which spans the Thompson River at the edge of the village. A slow-moving work train had run over the children as it backed into Lytton from a worksite just up the river.

Within a few minutes the two doctors who lived and worked in Lytton were in the operating room working on the little victims of this latest disaster and one of the doctors took a moment to tell us that there was a vague possibility that the missing limbs could be surgically re-attached but only if the severed pieces were found immediately and stored in ice. After finding out the

Both children and trains are somewhat unpredictable. The combination of the two demands awareness and focused adult supervision in order to avoid tragedy.

Kids and Trains

approximate location of the incident in relation to the length of the bridge, we ran back to the car and raced to the bridge. As we drove we radioed back to our office to request a supply of clean containers and ice in the event we were able to recover some of the severed limbs.

One small thing in our favour was the fact that the children had not been far enough out on the bridge to be over the water. The bridge was built of timber and steel and was quite high above the water but it also spanned about one hundred metres of dry land between the river's edge and the rock of the canyon wall. The deck consisted of wooden railway ties lying across the main beams of the structure with the steel rails spiked onto these cross-ties but the spaces between the cross-ties would allow any small objects that dropped onto the bridge to fall through to whatever was below. My partner ran out onto the bridge to find the exact location where the children had been struck while I made my way down into the brush and brambles below. After we established the location where we would conduct our search, my partner joined me in the frantic search for body parts. Soon another policeman from the office joined us, bringing buckets and ice and plastic bags. Over the next hour we found tiny hands and feet with various lengths of arm and leg attached. As each part was found, it was placed in ice and kept out of the sunshine as much as possible. The hospital staff had provided us with an estimate of the total number of limbs that were missing but we had no way of knowing if any one part had been severed more than once. After about an hour of searching we were scratched and bruised and dirty but we were fairly certain that we had all that was there and we took our collection to the hospital.

On arrival there we saw one little body lying on a stretcher at the side of the room; it was completely covered with a white sheet and there was no movement. There were two little survivors, a girl and a boy, and we were told that the dead child was a girl who had been the twin of the surviving girl. The doctors were about finished with the crushing emergency that had been presented to them and one of them told us that he had been in touch with surgical experts at a major Vancouver hospital and they had confirmed what he and his partner had reluctantly concluded: the nature of the crushing wounds delivered by the wheels of the train made it impossible to re-attach the missing limbs. We had all tried but failed.

These three small children had been playing near their homes on the reserve when for some unknown reason they decided to make their way over the short distance to the railway tracks. The supervising parents had not noticed they were gone until it was forever too late.

The work train consisted of a locomotive and two or three flat cars with an old passenger coach at the rear to serve as a place for the workmen to ride and take breaks from their labours. As the train had been reversing into town, the old coach, in which several workers were riding, had been the lead unit. As the train rounded the curve and was about to cross the river the workmen were looking out the coach's end doorway and saw the children on the bridge. They immediately ran back into the car to activate the train's emergency stop mechanism but it was then far too late to stop the slowly moving mass and they all watched in horror as the coach and at least one of the flat cars passed over the spot where the children had been sighted. As soon as the train came to a stop the workers scrambled down from the coach and made their way back along the bridge. What they found there will have been etched in their minds for the rest of their lives. They gathered the children in their arms and ran with them to the nearby hospital.

Since that terrible day the two surviving children struggled with their awful handicaps. The girl has lived her entire life in Lytton where she raised a family of her own and is now a grandmother.

A Native Rancher

This story comes out of the beautiful Botanie Valley that drains into the westward-flowing Thompson River about a mile before it joins the southbound Fraser River at Lytton. "Botanie"—pronounced "boat-ann-ee"—is a word from the language of the Nlaka'pamux people who have lived in that region for at least ten thousand years and it means something like "cloud on the mountain" or "blanket of cloud." As a child, Johnny McIntyre saw the beauty and potential of this valley during visits there with his parents and when still a boy he formed the idea of living and ranching there one day.

However, the government had long ago given much of the land in the Botanie Valley to the Anglican Church as an incentive to the church to establish a Native residential school near Lytton. The land grant included a large part of the valley floor and ran up both sides of the valley nearly to the timberline; several freshwater springs bubbled up near the foot of the protective mountains on both sides. A public road allowance passed through the land along the creek at the approximate mid-line of the property and on either side lay natural hay meadows with great potential for cattle grazing. Interestingly, a condition of the grant was that if the residential school was ever closed, the granted land was to become part of the territory of the Lytton Native band.

Few of the school's administrators and teachers, who came from all over the world, had the necessary experience and skills to manage a "cow-calf" operation and over the years they struggled with the potential of the property. Unfortunately, this lack of experience coupled with their short-term appointments doomed it to be a rather marginal and mostly unsuccessful operation. Finally the decision was made to find someone who could dedicate all the necessary time, skill and effort to develop a successful cattle operation there. Johnny McIntyre jumped at the opportunity to live and work in the beautiful valley that he had loved since his childhood and in due course he was selected for the job and a contract was drawn up that allowed him to call the shots on almost every aspect of the proposed cattle operation.

One of the first things that Johnny undertook as ranch manager was to fence the hay meadows on the valley floor to keep the summer grazing cattle away from their winter feed supply. After fencing, these meadows produced enough feed most years to carry the small herd through the winter without buying any from outside sources. This project was only one of the steps that clearly showed Johnny's ambition and understanding of cattle ranching and his will to do whatever would improve the overall operation. He became a hard-working and dedicated rancher and soon many of the Lytton band members found employment on the ranch, helping with the haying operations and fence construction and repairs or the many other labour-intensive jobs that must be attended to on a working cattle operation. And after a time the Botanie ranch operation came to be known among the locals as the "McIntyre Ranch."

A Native Rancher

During the years that I worked as a policeman at Lytton, the McIntyre ranch and its operator were little known among the non-Native people of the area. Johnny worked on the land from daylight to dark almost every day from spring to late fall and attended to the feeding and oversight of the herd every day throughout the winter. Like many of the farmers from my home district in Alberta, he found that taking a holiday or even necessary travel-time away from the ranch was a difficult undertaking because many years of toil and pride were at stake if anything out of the ordinary was to occur in his absence. Although he had a few workers he had come to trust over the years, even the best of hired hands could not be expected to be as involved and caring about the welfare of the overall project as Johnny McIntyre.

Then one summer night during the second year of my time in Lytton I was on a routine patrol when I encountered an old pickup truck on a secondary road. It was moving noticeably slower than average traffic and it wandered continuously during the short time that I watched it. I could see that the driver was slouched behind the steering wheel and he showed no awareness of my marked police car. I immediately suspected that the driver of this vehicle was drunk and I finally got his attention through the use of my siren and flashing lights. The vehicle came to a gradual stop.

I jumped out of the police car and was beside the suspect vehicle almost immediately. I was shocked and saddened to recognize the driver as Johnny McIntyre and he was displaying all the classic symptoms of an impaired driver. He was genuinely remorseful about the foolish error he had made but it was then too late. He told me that some old friends had stopped by the ranch during the evening with a bottle of whisky. One drink led to another but unfortunately none of them had passed out from their indulgence. Johnny had then made the bad decision to attempt the short drive from the ranch to his home, which was just south of Lytton below the highway.

At that time I was still very dedicated to doing my duty "without fear, favour or affection." I regretted what I felt must be done but there was no alternative for me. I arrested Johnny and dealt with the circumstances as I had done with many other people in similar situations. He appeared in the local provincial court in due course and pled guilty to the charge of impaired driving. The magistrate treated him in the same manner as anyone else: a fine of about two hundred dollars and a thirty-day suspension of his driver's licence.

I had not been Johnny McIntyre's close friend or associate before this incident, though we had known and recognized each other, but after the impaired driving charge our encounters in the little community were tension-filled and difficult and we took to avoiding each other. As he was an outstanding member of the community I really regretted this outcome.

It was about a year after this incident with Johnny McIntyre that an excited motorist came into the RCMP office early one afternoon to report a fire in the tinder-dry forest along the east canyon wall about eleven kilometres south of Lytton. Throughout the hot summers the Fraser Canyon generates an amazingly powerful upstream wind almost every day, a wind so strong and constant that the trees on exposed parts of the canyon walls have been forced to grow with almost no limbs on their downwind side. We all knew very well that this wind would fan a fire out of control in a very short time if it was not put down immediately.

At the first sighting of smoke the local Forest Service people had put out a call for help and soon received word back that the nearest water bombers were en route but they were coming from Kamloops, a distance of about 160 kilometres. The hour spent waiting for the air strike seemed more like a day but the two old World War II Avengers finally roared overhead, led by a smaller spotter aircraft. Every eye in the little community was on the spotter as the pilot made two runs over the fire to determine the

A Native Rancher

Motorists on the Trans-Canada Highway and the entire surrounding community watched as the wind-fanned fire began a terrifying march up the Fraser Canyon and toward Lytton.

best strike approach for the heavily loaded and cumbersome old bombers. Then at last the bombers began their attack and within a minute or two they had emptied their loads over the leading edge of the fire. There was a huge cloud of steam, smoke and ash. For a moment the strike appeared to have quelled the fire but the next few minutes made it very obvious that this was not the case and we watched as the wind-fanned flames began to jump from the top of one ridge to the next. The only reloading facilities for the water bombers were at Kamloops, which meant that they could not make another strike for about two hours, and it was very obvious that there would be no point in that.

The hottest part of the day was still ahead of us and we were now faced with a crisis. There were seven or eight homes scattered along the east wall of the canyon above the Trans-Canada Highway and between Lytton and the starting point of the fire. Five of these homes were destroyed in the next two or three hours. There were many more homes and buildings along the canyon wall below the highway, however, and our best possibility for saving them was to prevent the fire from crossing the road. By this time the canyon wind was carrying burning embers and flaming bits of debris ahead of the fire into the doomed area above the highway but a few missiles were also swirling downward and across it. Each time an ember found dry grass or pine needles, the Forest Service people attacked it with portable water tanks and hand-operated sprayer pumps.

We had put out a request for the highway to be closed at Hope and at Spences Bridge but even when this was done we were left with the traffic that was already into the 145 kilometres of road between the barricades. With the help of Department of Highways crews we then established local roadblocks above and below the rapidly expanding fire and I began patrolling the fire area to assist anyone who may have been caught in there.

As I patrolled I saw Johnny McIntyre working feverishly around his home just below the highway, attempting to reduce the fire hazard around the building. He had felled some trees on the upwind side of the house and was in the process of dragging them away with a small tractor. I stopped and helped him hitch the tractor to the trees then gathered dry grass and pine needles to pile within the spray pattern of the garden sprinklers that were wetting down the homesite from his very limited water supply. All this was done without an exchange of words, Johnny and I working together at the obvious tasks until some other men arrived to help. I then returned to my patrol duties.

In the early hours of the wildfire the entire village was under a constant shower of burning embers, and without immediate attention any of these could have become a disaster, but by nightfall the fire had passed above the community and was burning vigorously about fourteen kilometres up the Thompson River. The danger hadn't passed, however, as hot spots continued to blossom in the burned-over area and as each hot spot came to life there was a new source of flying embers, requiring an all-out attack. With the cooling of the evening the winds died down somewhat but few if any of the residents of Lytton got any sleep that night. Fortunately, over the next week the fire finally burned itself out of fuel and was brought under control.

Johnny McIntyre's home was spared along with all the others situated below the highway. Afterwards, the people of Lytton banded together to assist all those who had lost their homes and possessions that night and life in the canyon community continued as it had over the many years before the big fire.

A Professional Thief

In the spring of 1972 my family and I moved from Lytton to Golden. At that time the forest industry was in full bloom in Golden, and as anyone willing to work could immediately find a job, people were moving there from all over the Prairies and BC. New houses were springing up on every available residential lot and a complete new housing development was underway as well in an attempt to meet the demand for homes.

Boom times always bring problems and growing pains to any town, however. This is particularly true from the police point of view because the criminal element likes to be where things are happening and where money and merchandise are on the move. Any con artist or drug dealer who is worth his salt can make big money when his victims have a large and constant income.

And so it happened that the news of the Golden boom reached the ears of a very large and physically powerful Vancouver man—I will call him Valder Glib—whose constant criminal activity was beginning to generate police interest there. Mr. Glib

A Professional Thief

had a variety of criminal talents but his specialty was theft and he took great pride and satisfaction in never having anything in his possession that he had legitimately bought and paid for. In those few situations where he could not accomplish the acquisition of something he desired or needed by theft he would buy it with someone else's money.

Police interest is something that no full-time criminal enjoys or wishes to deal with, however, and having heard of Golden's boom he moved there to get a piece of the action. Fortunately, even seasoned and professional criminals make mistakes and Mr. Glib was no exception to this unwritten rule; his mistake was in underestimating Golden's back-woods police talent. It happened that among his stolen possessions was a powerful snowmobile, which he had been using for recreational riding in the abundant alpine areas around Golden. When this machine was in need of some minor repairs and servicing, he delivered it to the repair shop in Golden with all the outward confidence of one who was the machine's legitimate owner.

The Canadian Police Information Computer (CPIC) was new to us at that time and all our street and highway members were encouraged to make maximum use of it. We also established a policy of running the licence numbers of every car parked at the town's many motels each night. It was an activity that did not require a great effort on our part but the results were amazing: nearly every night these checks uncovered some criminal activity or a missing person or simply someone travelling on the Trans-Canada Highway for whom we had an urgent message from a family member. During our first full year with this new equipment the Golden RCMP detachment located and dealt with more occupied stolen vehicles than all other police units along the Trans-Canada Highway west of Calgary.

Then one day one of our motivated constables happened into the local snowmobile dealer's place of business on some matter and while there he routinely called in the serial numbers on each of the snowmobiles in the repair shop. The Glib machine was immediately identified as having been stolen during the previous winter from the back of a truck in Whistler, BC. Fortunately, Mr. Glib had been so confident of his anonymity in his new location that he had provided his correct name, address and telephone number on the work order. As we were more than a little surprised at this development, we held a mini-conference in our office to decide how we should handle the new information.

The repair shop was operated by a trustworthy man who was a long-time resident of the community and he gladly co-operated with us when we told him the circumstances. With our coaching, he called his new customer to advise him that the machine needed some replacement parts, which he would have to order from his out-of-town supplier. This ruse bought us a few days for further investigation before we would have to tip our hand.

We made a discreet patrol past the rented home that Glib had identified on the work order for the stolen machine. In the driveway was a flashy new four-wheel-drive vehicle and a check showed that it was registered to our suspect. A small flat-deck trailer sat in the carport with another snowmobile on it. The remainder of the carport was filled with boxes similar to those used in the moving industry. Normally neither the trailer nor the snowmobile would have interested us but everything now pointed to them probably being stolen as well. We could hardly contain ourselves in our desire to get their serial numbers.

Meanwhile, computer messages and telephone calls concerning our suspect had been flowing continually between our office and a variety of police offices in the Vancouver area. We had found several previous convictions for fraud and false pretences but as Glib's specialty was theft we were not surprised to learn that there were several offences on his record for both theft over two hundred dollars and theft under that amount. Conversations

A Professional Thief

with some of the officers who had investigated past Glib offences indicated that this man was a very, very active thief and one of the previous investigators was quite convinced that everything in the man's home was stolen property.

Two days after the initial discovery at the snowmobile shop we approached the local magistrate with an application for a search warrant for the Glib household and outbuildings. The warrant was granted immediately because those were the days when the administrators of the law believed that if something walked like a skunk, looked like a skunk and smelled like a skunk, it was logical to assume that it was in fact a skunk. This was also long before Canada's criminal element was granted the huge protection of the Charter of Rights. In today's court system it is highly unlikely that a warrant would have been issued at that point and if it had been it would have been vigorously attacked by defence counsel and very likely ruled to be a violation of the rights of the accused. The entire case for the crown would then have been on very shaky ground.

Early the next morning three of us arrived on the Glib doorstep with the search warrant plus a warrant for Mr. Glib's arrest. While one of us dealt with him at the door, the other two were all over the trailer and second snowmobile, and they had no difficulty finding serial numbers on both of them. We called the numbers in to the office where they were entered into CPIC and there they were! Both were listed as stolen property! We were totally amazed that this man who was an experienced and very bold thief had not made any effort to remove or obliterate the serial numbers. It was like shooting fish in a barrel!

From the get-go Mr. Glib was in total denial mode. He registered shock and disbelief that he should be suspected of theft—or any other offence for that matter! How, he asked, could a bunch of incompetent cops come to such an incorrect conclusion? The ridiculousness of the whole thing was almost more than he could bear!

We showed him the arrest warrant, gave him the required warnings and advised of his rights. It was during this process Mr. Glib told us that after a disagreement just that morning his wife had packed up her things and taken a bus back to Vancouver. He even displayed a few tears during the telling of this heart-breaking tale. By this time we were all agreed that this fellow should have found a career in Hollywood. Sympathy is a rare commodity among police when they are dealing with such people, but before we took Mr. Glib away to our cells one of our guys suggested that if Glib felt a genuine need for sympathy, he should look in the section of the dictionary between "shit" and "syphilis."

As soon as he and his police escort arrived at our office Mr. Glib made his rightful call to a Vancouver lawyer. Over the next ten days I marched our suspect to the courthouse every day and every day he was released by the magistrate to appear at a later date to enter a plea and continue the process. Each day as he reached the door of the courthouse we re-arrested him on new information we had garnered from the search of his home and vehicles. Although we were now convinced that everything he had in his possession had been obtained by crime, we could only identify a few items sufficiently to lay charges but these included the two snowmobiles, the trailer, numerous shop and power tools, a washer and dryer, a very large television set, and a beautiful, high-quality leather recliner chair.

This chair was the subject of an amusing story. A sharp-eyed policeman in the Vancouver area was scanning our computer-generated list of suspect items when he noticed the details about the chair. He had recently received an unusual theft report from a high-end furniture dealer. A large and powerful man (a description that fit Mr. Glib perfectly) had entered the store and browsed among the displays until he suddenly picked up the heavy recliner chair and staggered toward the door with it. One of the sales people had hurried over to hold the door open for this self-help

A Professional Thief

customer and he was gone before they realized they had been victimized. The helpful sales person was positive he could identify the man who had carried the chair away and the chair itself was unique enough that we were confident it could be positively identified to the court. With the help of these bits of information Mr. Glib was required to spend another night with us.

Each day the list of offences grew longer and Mr. Glib and his lawyer became quite frustrated with our *Columbo*-like methods of dealing with them. It was immediately after the fourth re-arrest that the lawyer called me, threatening a lawsuit if I continued this course of action. Now it was my turn to put on the Hollywood performance. I explained carefully how awful we felt about having to re-arrest this poor fellow on so many occasions but as long as the information kept coming to us in bits and pieces we had absolutely no choice. I then pleaded with the lawyer to advise his client to tell us about the sources of all his possessions so that we could get on with all the charges in a single batch. The lawyer, however, did not consider this to be a constructive suggestion. I concluded my performance by telling the lawyer that he should then advise his client that this process could go on all summer.

The information stream gradually slowed to a trickle and at last Glib was released on a bail arrangement to appear later for the purpose of entering his plea. The process then dragged on for six months or more until, with no options left, Glib and his lawyer appeared in court to enter guilty pleas to all charges. He was sentenced to eighteen months in the provincial jail for the theft of the Whistler snowmobile and concurrent sentences on all the remaining offences. All the identified stolen goods were eventually returned to their rightful owners. Tragically, we had been unable to positively identify a great many other items we had seized from the Glib house so they had to be returned to him after he was released from jail.

Some days are diamonds. Some days are stone.

A Missing Aircraft

We were into late spring in the valley where the town of Golden lies. For me this was always a favourite time of the year—although fresh leaves were growing rapidly in the local forests, we could still go cross-country skiing in the mountain passes on either side of town, Kicking Horse to our east and Rogers to our west. Sometimes a rain storm in the valley could add a few inches of fresh heavy snow in the high country and the ski experience would be new again. However, at the outset of this story the weather had suddenly warmed up. There had been a couple of days of heavily overcast skies and almost constant rain and now the mountain snows were quickly turning to water. Those of us who enjoyed the high country skiing experience had mixed feelings about this but we'd had a good long ski season and knew it could not go on much longer.

On the morning of the third day of wet weather we learned that two young men had left Calgary in a small aircraft bound for Kelowna, a two-hour flight, and had failed to arrive at their

A Missing Aircraft

destination. The pilot had reported his intention of following the Trans-Canada Highway to the north end of the Okanagan before turning south along the Okanagan Highway to Kelowna. The missing craft's last reported position was west of Banff.

Our first task was to check the airstrip at the edge of town to verify that the craft had not landed there and failed to report. With this done, we were left with nothing to do except wait. Our local weather was still too closed in to allow for an air search and most of the backcountry roads were closed for the breakup season. However, the next morning dawned bright and sunny and the air search was on. Search efforts were to be based in Golden where there was an adequate paved landing strip and a readily available fuel supply. The first craft to arrive were the fixed-wing aircraft from the Search and Rescue Centre at Comox and after a series of quick passes along the entire length of the flight plan from the last confirmed location to Kelowna they began searching in a grid pattern. They were soon joined by a large twin-rotor

The Rocky Mountains west of Jasper include Mount Robson, the guardian of the Yellowhead Pass and the tallest of the Canadian Rockies.

helicopter from the Comox base; volunteer private aircraft and spotters from Calgary to Kelowna also joined the search.

When I spoke with some of the crew on these aircraft, I found them quite sure they would locate the missing plane in a short time because of the almost perfect visibility over the entire search area. They explained that an aircraft crashing in a forested area will almost certainly break off a tree-top in its final moment of flight and this freshly broken tree will stand out like a flag in the overall carpet of green below the search planes. As a search goes on, the areas are over-flown at different times of the day because the afternoon sun may show a broken tree that the morning sun did not.

But in spite of the original optimism of the searchers, the search dragged on for days. During this time the fixed-wing military aircraft from Comox would return to their home base at the end of each day but the slower double-rotor helicopter would set down for the night at the Golden airstrip. During the first days of the search a police car would provide a ride for the helicopter crew to their motel accommodation at the other end of town. Then they discovered a bit of a field behind the motel where they were staying and decided to park their craft there, an arrangement that would allow them to be in search mode almost an hour earlier each morning. Those were the days when it was still possible to park a military aircraft in some secluded location without the need for an armed perimeter guard so this was definitely a win-win situation as it also relieved us of the need to provide a ride for the crew.

The plan worked flawlessly until the third evening when the big machine glided in over the little field behind the motel and settled onto the ground. The pilot cut the power and the machine was in shut-down mode when the earth gave way beneath it and its front end tipped into a big hole in the ground—an unused septic tank that had served the motel prior to the town sewer system reaching the area. The motel business had changed hands a short time before this event and no one in the area had remembered the existence of this trap. Under the careful guidance of military engineers, local construction equipment was used to lift the machine out of the hole and after a careful assessment it again flew away. The crew members felt they had been very lucky: had the front end of the machine dropped only a few inches more the still turning main rotor would have bitten into the ground and caused serious or total destruction of their machine.

Eventually the air search was called off but we continued to hope that when loggers returned to the forest after the spring breakup, the plane would be found but this did not happen. It was not until mid-October that year that we learned the fate of the two young men and their plane. A horse-mounted big game hunting party had made its way into a creek valley in the Kootenay Mountains about twenty-four kilometres to the south and east of Golden when they found the almost completely burned-out remains of the little aircraft. It lay in the narrow upper reaches of the valley in a thick stand of evergreens. Neither of the men in it could have survived the crash and the fire that must have immediately followed.

None of the local pilots or any of us at the police office ever learned the reason for the young men's attempted flight to Kelowna but speculation always runs wild after an incident like this one. Some of the pilots said that the somewhat inexperienced young man at the controls of the doomed aircraft should not have even considered the trip in the weather conditions that day. They speculated that somewhere around Lake Louise he had seen a rain or snow squall ahead and in order to cross the continental divide had detoured to the Vermillion Pass to the south. Then something along this route had caused him to try another variation from his flight plan and he had flown in a northwesterly direction, attempting to get back to the Trans-Canada Highway at a point east of Golden. Partway along this course he had become disoriented by the limited visibility and turned into the fatal creek valley. The little airplane had struggled to gain altitude but the valley floor was rising faster than the plane was able to rise. Suddenly the pilot must have realized that the sides of the valley had closed in on him and he had been forcing it into a very tight turn when it lost flying speed and crashed to the snow-covered canyon floor.

The falling plane had not broken either treetops or limbs because it had sliced sideways into the heavy forest to the crash sight. And although the fire from the remaining gasoline and limited other combustible material on the plane had burned hotly, the fire had not spread into the trees because the forest was extremely wet and rain was likely falling at the time of the crash. As a result, from the air the crash site was invisible.

Golden Flying Deer

Golden is famous for its annual snowfall and the winter of 1974–75 was certainly not a disappointment to the local snow lovers. Even before Christmas, avalanche conditions were building in the mountains on both sides of the little community—in Rogers Pass to the west and Kicking Horse Pass leading east into Alberta. The major avalanches would come a little later in the season but the deep powder snow was already sloughing off the more local slopes and causing havoc on the railway and the highway.

Frequently snow sloughs would delay the Canadian Pacific trains enough that their crews would have to be replaced at the end of their shift-times when the train was still twenty or thirty kilometres outside of Golden. In these situations the local Golden Taxi Company would be called to take the replacement crew out and bring the relieved workers back to town. These crew transfers were made possible by the geography of the area that had forced the railway and the Trans-Canada Highway to use the same valley routes through the mountainous terrain.

TRAGEDY ON JACKASS MOUNTAIN

The beautiful community of Golden lies where the Kicking Horse River meets the Columbia River. This summertime vista is from Mount 7 and the beginning of Rogers Pass is in the background.

This closeness meant there were a number of locations along the routes where the crews could make their way through the snow to and from the stalled railway trains and the taxis waiting for them on the highway.

Without the railway business the Golden Taxi Company, which was a one-man show run by a long-time member of the community, would not likely have come into existence but these problem times on the railway meant the owner frequently had to work some very long shifts. At times the demand for the taxi service was so large that he had to hire other drivers to give himself a few hours of sack time. One of those most frequently called on to do some relief driving for the taxi company was another of the long-time local citizens. This man—I will call him Peter—was a good choice for this purpose as he was nearly always "between jobs" and was therefore available for piece work. At that time a person wishing to become a taxi driver was required to have local police approval and although Peter did not have an impeccable reputation with the police, he seemed to be quite capable of driving in a safe and law-abiding manner. As a result, he had been able to obtain this endorsement for a number of years. He took great pride in this and in spite of the very adverse winter conditions around Golden he was seldom if ever involved in vehicle impacts or collisions. He was truly happy when driving a taxi because he reveled in the gratitude of the people he carried to and from their work under these often difficult conditions.

It was about 10 p.m. one very dark night a few days before Christmas that Peter was called to take some replacement railway people up the Kicking Horse Canyon to the first point where the highway and the railway came close enough to allow a crew transfer. He expected to take four workers to the train and bring another four back to Golden and in due course he delivered the replacement crew to the chosen location. However, for some unknown reason there were no people there to be brought back to town. Fate must have intervened and these workers must have caught a ride with a friend or relative or with one of the many railway service vehicles that were frequently on the highway. Peter was left to return alone down the Kicking Horse River Canyon to Golden.

At that time the first eight kilometres from Golden up the Kicking Horse River Canyon to the east were said to be the absolute worst part of the Trans-Canada between the Atlantic and the Pacific oceans. The grade was severe, there were numerous sharp curves and the road surface comprised just two minimum-width lanes with absolutely no shoulders. The first step over the guardrail on the open side of the road would take you down one hundred to three hundred metres toward the river and in many places the inside or the rock-side of the highway rose vertically about an equal distance straight up. On the benches and crags of these rocky walls there were nearly always a variety of big game animals—mostly deer but also elk, mountain goats and big horn sheep.

That night a few of us were sitting around in the police office in Golden when we heard a lot of vocal commotion on the street out front. Someone was shouting loudly and somewhat incoherently. Several of us immediately went out to see what this was all about and we found Peter standing beside his severely damaged taxi and yelling wildly about something flying in the river canyon and landing on his car. The hood of the car had been crushed down until it was in close contact with the engine. The windshield was also crushed on the passenger side but the plastic inner layer of the window had prevented penetration by whatever had hit the car. The roof of the car had been bashed downward several inches and the rear window had exploded into thousands of pieces as it was designed to do under severe stress. Peter also appeared to have nearly exploded into little pieces himself but he had managed to control the car throughout his adventure and had driven directly to the police station where he really did go to pieces. His loss of control was quite understandable but he was so overcome by what had just occurred that he wasn't making much sense. Flying deer?

We kept asking Peter what had happened and where it happened and if he had suffered any injury. At last his bellowed response was that it had happened a few kilometres into the Kicking Horse Canyon and that he was hit by two flying deer and that he did not think he was injured. One of our guys did a closer examination of the damaged taxi and, sure enough, he was able to see traces of deer hair and blood on the damaged areas of the car. He got Peter's attention briefly and with a serious look, he asked, "Did you also happen to see a tiny red sleigh and a fat man with a white beard?"

Peter gathered himself to respond to the question, and after a long moment of thought, he replied, "No! I just seen the one that hit the window and I heard the one that hit the roof."

Golden Flying Deer

We were all quite relieved to know that Santa had not been involved.

A patrol into the canyon revealed the remains of three mule deer near the base of a vertical section of the mountainside that rose steeply away from the highway. Apparently two of them had landed on the passing taxi and the third hit the highway surface just behind the cab. All three must have died on impact as they had to have fallen about one hundred metres. We did not have the ability, equipment or the inclination to climb up and see what could have caused such abnormal behaviour among these deer but afterwards several old-timers and the conservation officer speculated that they had very likely been spooked by a cougar or wolves and had chosen suicide over being bitten and clawed to death.

Peter gradually gathered himself together as our conversation and investigation went along and he began to see the humour of it, laughing with us about the Santa Claus aspect of the story. Another Kicking Horse River Canyon incident was over and done with and fortunately this time only the deer had been killed.

Bugaboo Helicopter Skiing

During the mid-1960s, a group of dedicated mountaineers gathered sufficient financing to open a helicopter skiing operation in an amazingly beautiful area of the Purcell Mountains to the south and west of Golden. The centre of their operations was a beautifully constructed log lodge at the foot of the valley below the Bugaboo Glacier. Road access to the lodge consisted of about forty-eight kilometres of steep and winding gravel road, which left Highway 95 at Spillimacheen. The road had been built by logging operators and at that time was still considered an industrial road, which meant that recreational vehicles were allowed to use it with the understanding that they would get the hell out of the way of any and all logging equipment.

The view from the lodge included the glacier, which fills the upper end of that valley, and the black granite spire that pierces the centre of the glacier and is locally known as the Hound's Tooth. Telescopes and binoculars were provided for summertime guests at the lodge so that they could watch climbers tackling the Tooth, a real challenge because of its smoothly polished sides. The big draw for this lodge, however, was the skiing, and although it was expensive to ski here, the lodge was completely booked for the season long before the first snowflake fell on the mountains in October and continued into early May.

The big helicopters used for the ski operation were based in Golden, about a half-hour's flying time from the lodge, and they would arrive at the lodge at first daylight to take guests to a grand variety of deep powder, extreme downhill skiing. Each helicopter carried ten or eleven skiers and an experienced guide, lifting them from the lodge to the start of their first run then picking them up at the bottom and lifting them to the start of the next. There were enough runs in the area that in ideal snow conditions a group seldom did the same run twice on the same day.

This skiing experience was not for the novice. Several of the available ski runs were in excess of eighteen hundred vertical metres from the helicopter drop-off point to the pick-up location. The runs were all given colourful names so the guides could easily keep the information centre in the lodge informed of their location. One of the most outstanding runs had been named by the English-speaking skiers who used it during the first year of the operation. They would step from the helicopter, strap on their skis and then make the few strides to where they could see the course they were about to enter. Almost without fail they would exclaim, "Holy Shit!" and that became the name of the run. Even the easier runs required lots of nerve and experience.

There were times, of course, when the mountain snow was unstable due to recent heavy falls or melting conditions and at such times some of the runs were too dangerous to be used. The guides and the lodge managers kept a constant watch on snow and weather conditions and each morning they held a meeting prior to the first flight to decide if special precautions were necessary.

Once on their way, the guide in each group was responsible for all aspects of the adventure. Skiers were told that no track or trail was to be entered without his approval; any violations of these rules could result in the skier spending the next day in the lodge.

All these precautions and rules were very necessary because of nature's unforgiving temperament. In fact, there are very few locations in these mountains where a person is not in some danger of avalanches or falling rocks and skiers know and appreciate these risks; most understand that nature may turn loose an avalanche at the wrong time and that if they are in its path they will most likely die. I am not a downhill skier but I can understand why people are willing to test their luck against the elements even in these conditions. The spectacular scenery and the thrill of unlimited powder snow will lead otherwise conservative people to be a little reckless.

It was during the last days of the spring skiing season that we received a call at the Golden RCMP detachment that there had been an avalanche in the Bugaboo ski area and five people were dead. Because the Coroner's Act requires and provides the authority for an investigation into every sudden death, I drove to the local airport and flew from there to the scene in one of the big helicopters. The pilot and I skimmed along just above the jagged tops of the Purcell Mountains until we came over a ridge from where we could see another helicopter sitting near the centre of a snow field. The avalanche had started on the slope above the helicopter and we could plainly see the tracks of a group of skiers leading into the slide area. These ski tracks intersected the slide path near its upper end, suggesting that the ski group had, in fact, triggered this slide, though it may have been just ready to go at the moment they arrived.

We landed near the other helicopter and headed for the people standing nearby. They were all tourists from Germany but most of them spoke English very well and I was able to gather

Bugaboo Helicopter Skiing

The Purcell Mountains and its glacier-filled valley of the Bugaboo are a heli-skiing destination. The rarely climbed Hound's Tooth spire pierces the Bugaboo Glacier.

the facts leading up to the slide. The guide leading the group had selected their route, though the melting snow conditions had forced him to stay higher on the shoulder of the mountain than he would have under better conditions. He and four of the skiers had just completed their crossing of the slide area when they heard the explosive sound of the snow breaking away behind them. They looked back in time to see five of the group being swept down with the avalanche but they were only able to watch as the doomed skiers struggled to stay on the surface of the concrete-like mass. Then, one by one, they went under. None resurfaced. Two skiers, the tail end of the group, remained on the other side of the slide path. Fate had left them just short of the sweeping destruction.

The avalanche was less than a kilometre in length, very short by mountain snow slide standards, but what it lacked in distance it made up in the weight of the partly melted snow that composed its mass. Even before it began to move, it was very heavy from the spring melt, and once it was underway, the snow mass compressed and became nearly as heavy as an equal volume of water. The incident was over in less than thirty seconds, the snow mass coming to a stop on the more gradual slope below the shoulder of the mountain, and in an instant it was so solid that a person could walk around on it and hardly leave a footprint.

The guide had called by radio for their helicopter to return immediately and then the survivors had skied down onto the fallen mass of snow, arriving near the middle of it just as the helicopter landed nearby. Each person in the ski group had carried one of the small radio transceivers that had been designed for persons to carry whenever they might be exposed to an avalanche. These units had been set to transmit their unique pulsating signal as each ski run began and now the five transceivers buried in the slide were transmitting their signals under the snow. The survivors switched their own radio devices to become receivers and they quickly located the transmitters within a few metres of each other.

The helicopters each carried ten stout snow shovels and a frantic effort began to dig the slide's victims out. This slide was more ice than snow and the shovels had to be driven deep into the surface on all four sides of each section of snow before it would break loose and could be thrown aside. Progress was slow in spite of the great effort put into the task and it was twenty minutes after the slide had stopped before the first body was lifted to the surface. There were no vital signs and the victim did not respond to attempts to revive him, though he had been trapped under less than one metre of snow. The next three were somewhat deeper, while the fifth was nearly two metres down.

The autopsy reports on the five bodies showed that each had died of asphyxiation; none of the bodies had broken bones and there were only minor scratches and abrasions. The would-be rescuers had done their best under difficult circumstances but the time for a successful rescue had been too short; the air supply had been cut off the moment each body became buried. Even if the victims' heads had been above the surface, when the mass stopped moving, breathing would have been extremely difficult. The coroner's inquiry concluded that the five had died accidentally and no blame was attached to any person, living or dead.

The Runaway Train

The decision to route the Canadian Pacific Railway through the Kicking Horse Pass must have been left to politicians because no one who cared or had any valid knowledge of the terrain would have chosen this route unless they were influenced by greed, stupidity, corruption, or all three. There were two better routes available. The main objection to the Yellowhead route was that it was too far from the border with the US, which may have been a valid concern at that time, but then the Crowsnest Pass should have been the logical choice. Its grades were much easier to manage, it gets much less snow and it lies close to the US border but for some unknown reason, the Crowsnest route was not used.

Having decided on Kicking Horse, the railway men then speeded up construction by building a temporary thirteen-kilometre line over Mount Stephen (3,199 metres), which lies east of Field, instead of blasting a tunnel through it to accommodate the rail line. The track left the Columbia River at Golden and followed the Kicking Horse River to Field where it suddenly rose in almost a straight line with a 4.5 percent rise (four and one half feet for every one hundred feet of track) over Mount Stephen to the summit of the continental divide. There were steeper grades in Europe and Asia but trains there were hauled up and down these grades by using cables or third rails with cog teeth and a traction gear on the locomotive. The Canadian Pacific, however, was operating with conventional steel on steel traction and its steam locomotives were designed for the maximum 2.2 percent grades usual in the rest of Canada.

    The CPR dealt with this situation for more than twenty years by building and buying specialty locomotives and using four of them—two pulling and two pushing—to move small eastbound trains up the hill from the settlement of Field. Fortunately, the heaviest trains in those times were headed from the Prairies to the Pacific with grain, coal or livestock for export and the problem then became one of holding the load back while lowering it over that mountain and avoiding a complete runaway. Numerous trains were wrecked on that hill and today cairns and point-of-interest signs show their locations. The problem was remedied to a great extent in 1907–09 by the massive construction job that created the spiral tunnels—two three-quarter circles of tunnel bored into Mount Ogden and the adjacent Cathedral Crags—that added 9.98 kilometres of track to the route and reduced the grade to 2.1 percent. It is a very interesting experience to watch a long freight train enter the mountainside and come out above itself only to cross the valley and enter another mountain and repeat this strange manoeuvre.

    On the other side of Golden the construction and maintenance of the railway through the Rogers Pass area of the Selkirk Mountains was equally difficult but compounded by an average annual snowfall of about twelve metres. Here too the original rail line was laid on the surface and crossed the summit below the Illecillewaet Glacier but the avalanche conditions were so severe in one section that the rail line had to be dug into a deep trench for one kilometre or more and then roofed over with very heavy timbers and covered with a layer of rock and earth about a metre deep. However, the force of the avalanches was often so great that the roof would be breached and the trench filled with snow, ice and rock. In the thirty years that the railway used this pass, 250 railroad workers lost their lives from avalanches and rock falls. The worst of these accidents occurred in the early spring of 1910 when an avalanche killed sixty-two men who were working on the rail line trying to clear a slide that had come down the previous day from the other side of the valley.

The sudden death of sixty-two men in one incident finally persuaded the CPR that something had to be done. Construction began on the 8.08-kilometre-long Connaught Tunnel under Mount Macdonald in 1913 and it was completed in 1916, shortening the rail route by almost seven kilometres. The Rogers Pass summit area was then allowed to return to its natural state

The Connaught Tunnel was forced through Mount Macdonald to take the CPR main line away from the avalanche danger of the Rogers Pass summit. Construction began in 1913 after 62 railway workers from Golden and Revelstoke died in a March 4, 1910, avalanche.

and it remained that way until the early 1960s when plans for the Trans-Canada Highway began to take shape.

Unfortunately, the Connaught Tunnel did not resolve all of the CPR's problems with that area. I was working at the RCMP detachment in Golden on November 26, 1977, when train #5820 crashed into the Illecillewaet River at the end of a runaway on the Revelstoke side of Rogers Pass. I well recall viewing the wreckage and marvelling at how all of the five-man crew had escaped with their lives.

This train was an extra on the line due to a larger than expected demand for coal in the Japanese market and it consisted of 106 coal cars, 7 locomotives, a robot car and a caboose for a total weight of 13,608 tonnes. The train had pulled into a siding just as it cleared the west exit of the Connaught Tunnel in order to allow an east-bound train to pass and to break out the four additional pusher engines that had helped to get #5820 up the east slope of the pass. The weather conditions were described as a blizzard but the signal system beside the tracks gave the all clear for the train to continue and the brakes were released to begin the sixty-five-kilometre downhill run toward Revelstoke, the steepest, most dangerous stretch of track in North America. An engineer in training was at the controls; beside him were the chief engineer and a brakeman. Another brakeman and a conductor were in the caboose, which was more than a kilometre from the head end of the train.

Within minutes after the train was back on the main track, the crew knew that they were in trouble. The maximum speed for this downhill run was thirty-two kilometres per hour but when the brakes were applied at twenty-four kilometres an hour, nothing happened. There were radio conversations between the caboose, the lead locomotive and the dispatch centre in Revelstoke. Meanwhile, the doomed train accelerated continuously until it was running at almost 130 kilometres per hour and in spite of everything the head-end crew tried nothing had any effect on the increasing speed. As they hurtled down the mountain, the head-end crew expected disaster as they entered each curve in the track. There was worse news, however, from the dispatcher up ahead: an east-bound freight was approaching from Revelstoke and its engineer had no choice but to speed up in hope of reaching the only siding that lay between the two trains. A head-on crash seemed inevitable.

In the caboose at the rear of #5820, the conductor had climbed outside and managed to open the coupling that held the caboose to the last coal car and he and the brakeman were now trying to bring it to a halt. Its manual braking system was activated by a vertical shaft at each end of the unit. On the top of these shafts was a wheel similar to the steering wheel of a car and turning it would mechanically force the brake shoes against the main steel wheels of the caboose. With the conductor at one wheel and the brakeman at the other they cranked until they could no longer move them but their efforts had very little effect. They were putting distance between the caboose and the racing train but their speed did not seem to be decreasing as they had hoped it would and they were in danger of colliding with the train ahead of them when it inevitably derailed. Each felt that the other had not done the correct thing at his end. They yelled at each other to do more and then ran through the caboose to swap ends but each was only able to gain an inch or less on the circumference of the wheels. So they swapped ends again and again. At last they realized that their efforts were having an effect, the caboose began to slow down and in a short time it came to a noisy halt. The sudden silence allowed them to hear the thunderous sound of the destruction of the train now one kilometre ahead of them.

Minutes after the caboose was disconnected, the head-end locomotives had hit the sharp curve leading onto the bridge over the Illecillewaet River and, four engines back, one of the huge train axles had snapped. That engine and the first carload of coal behind it took flight and crashed six metres down into the river. The rail tracks and ties were torn away by the broken axle and one after another the huge coal cars that made up the rest of the train jack-knifed and derailed to pile up in the river and along the tracks. Two robot engines in the middle of the train collided, spilling their diesel fuel supply, which ignited and set alight the engines and all the cars around them. Whatever fuel did not ignite was washed into the river.

But at the head-end of the train, the three lead engines were still on the track and the crew now discovered that, relieved of the uncontrollable weight of the train behind them, they were able to stop in a very short time. They had cheated certain death. They radioed to the approaching train and to Revelstoke to advise that the emergency was over. Back in the caboose the conductor and brakeman could not believe what they were overhearing. How could these head-end crewmen still be talking on the radio after the destruction they had just heard?

Seventy-eight coal cars were destroyed along with four locomotives and a robot car. The CPR immediately commandeered heavy crawler tractors and other equipment from wherever they could get them and set about getting the rail line back into service. Within ten days it was again carrying trains in both directions. The remaining cleanup went on for months on both sides of the crash site where the debris had been shoved in the fevered effort to reopen the line.

The total cost of that runaway train was estimated at six million dollars. The follow-up investigation by the Canadian Transport Commission (CTC) laid blame on the trainee driver, the brakeman in the first locomotive and the conductor in the caboose. The CTC found that the trainee had delayed his initial braking efforts until the train had reached twenty-four kilometres per hour and this had precipitated the chain of events that followed. Unaware of this miscalculation, he and the engineer had then released excessive amounts of brake pressure until there was not enough to counter the downhill momentum of the train. The conductor was faulted because he had disconnected the caboose, further depleting the brake pressure at precisely the time when the front-end crewmen were fighting for control of the train. However, all three were allowed to remain in the company's employ.

In 1984 the CPR called for tenders for the construction of another tunnel through the upper part of Rogers Pass. The 14.7-kilometre-long Mount Macdonald Tunnel, completed in 1988, is the longest railway tunnel in the western hemisphere. It lies ninety-one metres lower than the Connaught Tunnel, and as a result, the improved grades on this part of the rail line have allowed the company to dispense with the use of pusher locomotives to assist the heavy westbound trains. In the twenty years since its completion the tunnel has paid for itself in savings from these pusher operations alone. Today the Macdonald Tunnel is used mostly for westbound trains while the Connaught is used for the eastbound.

A Well-Oiled Trucker

It was early spring in the Columbia River valley between Golden and Donald Station but still late winter a few kilometres away in the much higher ground of the Rogers Pass. Snow was still falling there in abundance but this relatively warm snow was heavy and it quickly added weight to the critical masses that had accumulated over the previous months. As a result, the avalanche season was in full swing and hardly a day went by that Rogers Pass was not closed for at least a few hours to allow crews to clear another slide area. Fortunately, the major slides were very often carried across the highway by the many snow-sheds in the pass but the larger than average slides during that season often overflowed onto the highway at both ends of the sheds.

Whenever one of these large slides came down, the highway maintenance people in Golden would put up signs so that westbound highway users would have the option of taking the southern highway route or stopping in Golden to use the food and lodging facilities there. The same would be done for

TRAGEDY ON JACKASS MOUNTAIN

eastbound drivers at Revelstoke on the western end of the pass. The unfortunate folks who were already into the pass at the time of the slide would be stopped by a flagman and told they would have to wait out the slide-clearing process or turn back to either Golden or Revelstoke.

It happened that around noon one mid-week day a big one broke loose from a high point on the east slope of the pass and blocked the highway for several hundred metres to a depth of three to five metres. There was always a frenzied interlude after such an incident. Traffic immediately began to pile up on each side of the slide but as vehicles could not be left parked in established slide areas all available highways maintenance people would be put to work directing drivers to less hazardous locations. Only when this priority task had been accomplished could the road-clearing process begin.

Among the eastbound traffic caught in the pass on this occasion were nine tractor-trailer units, and their drivers were directed to park their rigs in the nearest and safest area to wait for the road reopening. Truckers are generally a gregarious lot and the nine men were soon visiting each other; cribbage games began in a couple of the trucks and just plain bull sessions in others. Among the unfortunate truckers caught that day was a fifty-year-old driver who operated between Vancouver and Calgary on a regular schedule. This fellow had been drinking to excess every day for more years than he could recall and in the process had developed an amazing tolerance for alcohol. Like most conditioned alcoholics, "Thirsty" had convinced himself that he had far more ability to handle alcohol than any other person on this Earth and tragically he was partially right. (Later he told me that he had been drinking a twenty-five-ounce bottle of hard liquor every day for as long as he could remember.) Over the years he had learned how to pass through police road checks and weigh scales and other routine stops without arousing any

A Well-Oiled Trucker

suspicion. He would have fit very nicely into the old saying, "I never knew he drank until the day I saw him sober."

Unexpected events, however, are the greatest enemy of folks like Thirsty and this snow slide was one of those events. Among the other delayed truckers was one of Thirsty's old friends and when these two recognized each other Thirsty was immediately invited over to his friend's truck where the driver began to rummage around in the sleeper compartment and soon found a part bottle of liquor. The highway maintenance people had suggested that the delay would be a few hours, and as these two had not met for a number of years, there was both time and good reason for a toast to old friendships. After the first one, Thirsty's friend could see no reason not to follow with another. Thirsty knew better but he was caught up in the moment and he could not think of a valid-sounding reason to turn it down.

The two men did not go to the unnecessary bother of measuring their drinks as such things are not done by real men. They poured their booze directly into coffee mugs and took it straight. Earlier Thirsty had only slept for a few hours at a point well west of the pass and on awakening had started his day like every other one with a long pull on his daily twenty-five-ounce bottle of whisky. Long years of experience and experimenting had taught him that after a pre-determined period of time he could allow himself another pull on the bottle, a workable routine that he had followed right up to a few minutes before the snow slide had forced him to stop.

Fate again reared its ugly head, however, when the road-clearing work went far better than the maintenance crew had expected and about the time the two old buddies had finished their second shot of liquor a workman came by in a vehicle to tell them that the road would be clear in a few minutes and the truckers should prepare to move out. This was good news for seven of the nine truckers but Thirsty and his old friend had some mixed feeling about it. The friend was no doubt on the edge of being impaired but Thirsty was far beyond that. He was by then falling-down drunk. Those two stiff drinks had taken his previously high blood-alcohol level to the danger point and he was now off his routine and out of control. By using all of his remaining concentration he returned to his truck where a small pull on his daily ration bottle was definitely in order to celebrate the success of making it there without going face-down in the snow.

When the signal came, the truck convoy moved out and started down the highway toward Golden, Thirsty's friend in the lead unit and Thirsty right behind him. From the moment they started out he was in big trouble, having difficulty with the simplest and most routine functions of driving. Each time he shifted a gear he would lose his focus on the road and the truck would wander wildly from side to side. Fortunately, he seemed to be aware of his great handicap and drove much slower than the road conditions would warrant, and very soon his friend in the lead truck, in spite of his borderline impaired condition, was out of sight.

The seven following trucks had no inkling of what had transpired at their forced stop and they were more than a little impatient at the pace Thirsty was setting. Then they began to notice that he was all over the road and both shoulders of it and waited for him to hit the ditch at the end of each of his swaying arcs. At last the convoy arrived at the point where their citizens' band radios could reach receivers in Golden and the police office there began receiving their calls. Although truckers will look after each other in many circumstances, all they wanted in this case was for Thirsty to be taken off the road immediately and they made no secret of that fact.

Al was in a patrol car on the Trans-Canada near the point where the highway crosses the Columbia River at the eastern end of the Rogers Pass. The necessary information was passed to him by radio at almost the same moment that he encountered the truck convoy with the wildly erratic truck in the lead. Immediately he turned his car and came in behind the erratic driver, all the time broadcasting on his radio what he was seeing as he followed the truck, trying to get the driver's attention with his lights and siren. "He's going off the road to the right," he reported then, "No, he's back!" "Now he's going off to the left." "Hey, he's back again!" This went on for several minutes until we heard, "Okay, he's done now. He's off to the right in a shallow muddy ditch and there is no coming out of that. I've got him now!" Our second patrol car arrived on the scene about the time Al had the stumbling drunk down out of his badly leaning truck cab. Another crisis was over and no one had died.

    Thirsty was arrested and brought to the Golden office where a breathalyzer test indicated a blood alcohol level that would be fatal to any but the most conditioned of alcoholics. He was lodged in our cells until the following day when he was taken before the court to plead guilty to charges of impaired driving and dangerous driving. He received a fine of several hundred dollars and his driver's licence was suspended for six months on each charge. I never heard anything more about Thirsty and his trucking career but I suspect that he was forced into retirement by the truck's owners, who would have had an understandable desire to keep their machines on the road.

Struck From Above

It was early fall 1978 after my transfer to the Quesnel detachment when rancher Hugh Gilbert came to the RCMP office to say that someone had shot five of his cows and left them to rot in the field. The incident had happened on Milburn Mountain about sixteen kilometres west of Quesnel near the building site of one of the earliest ranch operations in that part of the Cariboo plateau. The buildings had been abandoned for many years but Mr. Gilbert was still operating the ranch there.

I was working days and happened to be at the front counter to take the information from the irate rancher. Although he was a rather shy and quiet fellow, his anger was obvious from the way he presented the information to me and I had the impression that if he found the person who had done the shooting, that person would be in grave danger.

This was a good opportunity for me to get out of the office and see a part of the area that I had not visited. After I had written up the initial report, I asked how I would find my way to the site and when I could meet him there. As it was almost impossible to describe the route there due to the many forks and branches the road took as it made its way up the side of the mountain, the rancher said he would meet me where the trail branched off the Nazko road and I could follow him from there. We agreed on a time that would allow us both to have lunch and he then left the office.

About two hours later I was driving along the gravel road toward Nazko when I saw the rancher's four-wheel-drive pickup truck at the entrance to a side road leading onto the high ground to the right. As soon as he saw my car, Mr. Gilbert began driving at a brisk pace up the side of what was beginning to look like a real mountain. About one and a half kilometres up the road he slowed suddenly and turned onto a trail that climbed the mountainside even more steeply. His four-wheel-drive was now in its element and I knew it would be a struggle to stay with it in my vehicle, which was basically a conventional passenger car. I also knew that this rancher would not pass up an opportunity to show a cop how a real man drove in somewhat adverse conditions. I had grown up on an Alberta farm so I knew from experience exactly what he would have in mind by leading me up the hill at this record-setting pace. It would be a great story to tell his friends if he had to stop and come back to help me out of a jam due to my inferior driving ability, so I called on all my farm-boy driving skills and stayed with him for the entire six kilometres of really tough going. When we met at the end of our uphill battle, I stepped out of my car and, of course, did not even mention the drive up or the condition of the road. From that point on we communicated very well and I felt I had earned a degree of his respect.

Just beyond the point where the rancher had stopped his truck I could see the dead animals. They were obviously good quality Herefords (white-faced cows) and they had all been in excellent condition at the time of death. A mature fir tree stood in the middle of the string of dead animals, two of them very close to the base of the tree with two more beyond and one closer to our location, but all of them in a straight line. The remains of a very old page wire fence ran along beside the line of dead cows. This fence had obviously been abandoned for many years, and as the posts had rotted away, the wire had been crushed down until what remained of it was no more than a foot off the ground. The cattle would have been able to walk across it at any point they chose to do so.

Something about this scene did not appear to be the result of a shooting incident. Having shot a number of big-game animals over the years, I felt that the dead cattle were lying in unusual positions. There was also an accumulation of short ends of fresh green tree boughs lying in an approximate fifteen-metre radius around the big fir tree. Taking a wider view of the scene, I spotted a large piece of a tree-top about one hundred metres down the slope from the big fir tree, and examining it, I saw that it had been freshly broken off at a point where the trunk had been nearly fifteen centimetres. The break was at an angle across the thickness but appeared to have been crushed rather than just broken by wind or some unknown impact. Moving back farther from the cows and the tree, we could see that the broken tree top definitely came from that tree.

And then I knew. The cows had been killed by a lightning bolt. The energy had come down the tree to where it contacted the two cows closest to the base of the tree. It then followed the old fence wires in both directions from the tree and hit and killed the other three animals. The most unusual thing about this incident was that there was absolutely no indication of heat or fire and a close examination of the fence wires near the tree showed no fusing or melting in spite of the huge surge of electrical energy that must have come through them.

Perhaps this story will add something to the old farmers'

theories about hot and cold lightning bolts but whether it was hot or cold lightning that killed his cows Mr. Gilbert was at least relieved to learn how they had died. He was quite certain that his insurance coverage on the ranch provided for cattle losses due to natural occurrences but not for vandalism. He was therefore entitled to recover a portion of the loss and this knowledge was a comfort to him.

A Really Cool Driver

If my memory serves me well there were no winters in the central Cariboo during the time I was posted there that we did not get a session of extreme sub-zero weather and most years there were several of these events. Such weather was definitely not a new experience for me but I can still very well recall one my earliest winters there when the temperature did not rise above twenty degrees below zero for a period of six weeks during January and most of February. Weather events like this were usually accompanied by a fairly brisk north wind and little ice crystals could be seen falling from the sky at a forty-five degree angle. These little diamonds sting like wasps if they hit exposed skin and if they didn't sting you knew your skin was frozen and you had better get inside immediately.

In the course of one of these severe winters, we were blessed with a commander who adopted the detachment's unmarked car as his own, though it was intended to be available to any of our shifts or the specialty units for surveillance or similar duties.

A Really Cool Driver

Our commander lived a few kilometres outside of town and this was where the unmarked car was always located whenever he was not at the office or off to any number of other activities like grocery shopping or visiting friends. This unauthorized use of police equipment was the cause of much anger and discussion among the detachment peons and it was during one coffee break discussion of this matter that a diabolical plot began to form, a plot that would be relatively harmless but a wonderful teaching instrument.

The next day a member of the detachment visited the auto wreckers at the edge of town. Under the pretence of needing material for some sort of an experiment, he gathered a small plastic bucket full of glass fragments by smashing the case-hardened side windows of vehicles that were destined for the crusher. Case-hardened glass is that miracle material that under severe impact will break into thousands of rather harmless particles rather than the knife-like shards with razor edges that come from untreated glass. With this material in hand we were ready for the next stage of the plot: surveillance and waiting.

We all knew that our commander was a regular attendee at the curling rink and that the unmarked car was his regular mode of transportation to this activity. Through some nonchalant conversation around the office we learned the date and time of his next match there. The curling rink was located about five kilometres from the police office and nearly sixteen kilometres from our leader's residence, which was ideal for this plan.

Luck was with us in that, when the day of the curling event finally arrived, the extreme weather conditions that were necessary to the plot had not lessened but in fact may have become somewhat worse. Anticipation was at a peak around the office. Two perpetrators were selected from among those who were on duty that evening. Every detail of the plot was rehearsed in our minds and we were convinced that the operation would be flawless. Luck also provided us with a "mole" in the form of another policeman who was engaged in a curling match on the ice sheet right next to our illustrious leader. It now began to appear that fate was actually helping us with each phase of the plot. Our mole reported that the subject was engaged as we anticipated and that he would likely be there for the next two hours. We obtained the spare keys for the unmarked car from the secure storage location in the police office and the bucket of crushed glass from its secret storage location. All systems were go.

A marked police car rolled into the parking lot at the curling rink and stopped near the target car. People do not hang around in a parking lot when it is twenty or thirty degrees below zero so it was not a long wait until there were no witnesses to what was about to happen. Two men jumped out of the police car, opened the doors of the unmarked car and quickly wound down all four side windows so the glass was completely out of sight inside the doors. They then closed and re-locked the doors and scattered the crushed glass particles around and inside the car, being attentive to every detail so the evidence would be convincing. They were on their way again in less than five minutes.

The curling match came to the usual quiet conclusion and our mole left immediately as he had to deal with some urgent matters. Our commander attended the club bar to toast the results of the match and when all the celebratory drinks had been drunk and the after-match socializing was over he arrived in the parking lot to discover the vandalism to the parked police vehicle. His rage was quickly replaced by the realization that reporting this event would be extremely embarrassing at best and could result in a black mark on his service record at worst. He quickly came to the decision to replace the windows at his own cost.

He brushed away the glass particles from the driver's seat

with his mittened hand and slid into the car. He then drove the windowless car the five kilometres through the thirty-below-zero air to the back of the police office where he arrived in a near solid condition. He entered the office cursing and ranting about how he would deal with the vandals if or when he caught up to them. The only person in the office on his arrival was the lady known as Lou who acted as our cell guard and she was, of course, very sympathetic. A short time later she came on the radio to request an available car to give the boss a ride home and one of the men returned to the office and listened to the sad story of the vandalism while displaying his very best poker face. He assisted in placing a tarpaulin over the damaged car before taking the boss home to his out-of-town residence.

Early the next morning the boss arrived for work in his own car and his first order of business was to contact the glass shop in town to arrange for the replacement of the four side windows. The glass shop owner advised that replacing glass of this kind was very unusual and he would have to check his inventory but after a short time on hold he came back to say that luckily all four windows were on hand in his shop. Arrangements were made for the immediate repairs and the boss went for another windowless drive through the brisk winter air to the glass shop.

The car was immediately taken into the work bay and one of the employees began using a vacuum cleaner to clean up the crushed glass in the car interior while the manager prepared the paperwork. Before the two hundred dollar work order was completed, however, the two men in the office were interrupted by a yell from the work bay. The workman had discovered that the windows were completely undamaged. Not so the pride and self-esteem of our boss: he took the rest of the day off and went home. However, he did use his own car for all off-duty travel after that day and the events of the evening in question were never ever discussed.

A Tough Choice

Quesnel was a bustling community when I worked there in the early 1980s. On the date when this story took place I was in charge of the graveyard shift and we were into the second hour of what looked like a real barn burner of a night in the downtown sector. Fortunately, the detachment was actually up to full strength for a change and I had three constables on my watch. We lunged from one incident to the next as the liquor outlets closed after what must have been a very profitable night and the drunken crowd began to deal with the ugly fact that the party was coming to an end. Fist fights were so abundant that we only attended if we happened on them very near the outbreak but calls such as "Man down!" in the middle of a busy street were given priority because we did not relish the cleanup job if such events were not quelled immediately. The positive thing about a night like this was that the shift would be over before we realized it. Time flies when you're having fun!

On such nights I found the twenty-four-hour roadside

A Tough Choice

suspension to be of some functional purpose. We tried to be as visible as possible while we went about our duties in the hope that some of the potential impaired drivers would reconsider their need to drive. However, we were so overpowered by the sheer volume of calls from the alcohol-fuelled population that we could not spare the time to deal with impaired drivers unless they had run over someone or crashed into something and caused injuries. When one of us did encounter an impaired driver, we simply lifted the licence and advised its owner that he was under suspension for the next twenty-four hours. We would then tuck such licences into our notebooks and be finished with the incident in about ten minutes; the paperwork could be attended to when things slowed down later in the night. We knew very well that over half of these drivers would drive away as soon as we were out of sight but consoled ourselves with the knowledge we had done what we could.

These were the years of major progress in police radio communication systems all over BC and those of us who had worked with the earlier systems were pleased with the improvements because we had faced too many emergencies in complete isolation. Under the new system Quesnel was provided with two radio communication centres for police use, the one being in our own office and the second located about 120 kilometres away in the RCMP district administration centre at Prince George. On the rare occasions when we had no prisoners in our local lock-up and therefore no civilian prisoner guard-cum-office worker on duty, we could simply switch our telephone lines to the administration centre and communicate through them by using another radio frequency. A rather informal agreement also allowed us to make use of either radio centre during the late night or weekend hours.

On this night we did have prisoners in our lock-up and our prisoner guard was Lou, who was a most welcome addition to every shift that she covered. She had a wealth of local knowledge that many members relied heavily on during the early part of their postings there. She also used this knowledge to "sort the fly shit from the pepper" when she took phone calls to our office, so when she called on the radio and said we had a hot one, we knew that's exactly what we had.

It was about two that morning when Lou put in a call to all units to tell us that a woman had phoned to report that her drunken husband had just left their home with a loaded hunting rifle and an additional supply of ammunition. Lou had tried to gather as much information as she could about a possible motive but she had received mixed data. The caller stated that her husband was depressed and might be contemplating suicide but she also said that he had ranted about his dislike for some people. The wife did not know these people and could not even provide any names. Lou also learned that the suspect most likely did not have access to a vehicle.

Three of us scrambled into our cars and began speeding toward the area of the call. Moments later my fourth constable called to the central dispatch in Prince George to advise that he would be out of his car checking a motor vehicle. The location he gave was on the highway on the opposite side of Quesnel from the rifle call.

The firearms call had originated across the river from the business district in one of the residential developments, an area where our work seldom took us except to deal with traffic matters. The house in question was in the middle of a narrow strip of homes above the river's high-water mark and below a steep hill that rose away from the river. We placed a car at the upstream and downstream ends of this strip of homes while I attended at the residence and I was talking with the suspect's wife when we heard three rifle shots in quick succession. The sound caused the hair on the back of my neck to stand on end.

A Tough Choice

The shots seemed to come from somewhere behind the house in the area alongside the river but downstream from my location so the three of us regrouped closer to where they seemed to have originated. While one constable stayed with the cars, the second constable and I made our way cautiously toward the open gravel bar beside the river. We had to rely mainly on what we could hear as there was almost total darkness that night except for the bit of light that was coming from the business district across the river but it cast a glare on the water that impaired rather than helped our vision. Making our way to the edge of the scrub brush at the border of the gravel bar, we listened intently, though mainly to the pounding of our hearts. Suddenly we heard the sound of someone stumbling around among the rocks and gravel almost immediately in front of us and the constable and I moved a few metres apart to find vantage points above and below where we had heard the sound. We were now certain that someone was making his way along the edge of the gravel bar and that he was only a matter of metres away from us.

Then together we turned on our flashlights and illuminated our suspect. We had our man. He had been walking in the direction of his home and he was carrying a 30-30 Winchester rifle. We yelled at him to drop the rifle and raise his hands and told him we were the police. He stood motionless for a moment looking into the blinding glare of our flashlights while we tried to hold the lights steady in our left hands and our revolvers in our right. The moment seemed to go on forever until the man bent his knees and put the rifle down on the rocks at his feet. The crisis was over.

We placed the drunken man under arrest and handcuffed him. He was a long-time resident of the community and during the short ride to our office he apologized over and over for the foolish thing he had done. He had no explanation for why he was out in the dark with the rifle. Perhaps the cool fresh air had

TRAGEDY ON JACKASS MOUNTAIN

The Fraser River runs through the heart of Quesnel. A historic wooden bridge built in 1929—now a footbridge—is visible behind the vehicle bridge that connects the community.

sobered him a little but just as he had started for home again he had decided that it would be a good idea to fire a few shots into the air. He spent the night with us for being drunk in a public place. On his release in the morning he was issued a "promise to appear" on a charge of dangerous use of a firearm. I do not recall the result of the court appearance except that the man pleaded guilty to the charge. He was most likely dealt with by a fine and a court order not to possess firearms for a couple of months, which was a serious punishment as firearms were still considered a necessary tool in that part of the country.

As was often the case, the extreme street action of the early part of that night's graveyard shift had ended at almost the same time we were called to the firearms event. After booking our man into the cells, the three of us took a few deep breaths and headed for the local all-night coffee shop where we talked over what had happened and debated a bit about how such events could be handled better in the future. The most heated conversation

A Tough Choice

during our coffee break, however, concerned the whereabouts of our fourth man during the investigation. Almost immediately after we had called the office to advise that our suspect was in custody, we had heard a radio message to central dispatch advising that he was ten-eight—that is, back on the air and available. An examination of the radio log from Lou's desk and that from the central dispatch left no doubt about the sequence and timing of his "vehicle check."

    He remained conspicuous by his absence for the remainder of our shift and this absence became even more obvious after we all gathered in the office again to deal with the paperwork from our very busy night. As the first light of dawn entered the valley, I called for him to meet me in the office. It seemed to take him a long time to make his way there. His face looked ghastly and his posture defeated as he entered the main office and then immediately came into the side office where I was waiting for him. He closed the door and sank into the chair beside my desk. I asked him if he knew why I had called him in. Tears welled up as he acknowledged that he knew very well. I chose not to hammer him with the details of the earlier part of the shift but I did point out that we were all receiving equal pay for our work and that equal effort and commitment were an assumed part of that package. I then told him that he had a difficult decision to make but that in my estimation he was not suitably employed as a police officer. At the end of the interview I gave him a ride to the house he shared with his wife and two small children and told him to take whatever time he needed to decide how he was going to deal with his situation. I also advised him that my action in regard to his conduct would be greatly influenced by his choice.

    The graveyard shift the following night was the last of that sequence for my crew and the fourth constable called to say that he would not be in. Fortunately, we had a much quieter night than the previous one and we were then into our three days off. On my return for the next scheduled shift I learned that the fellow had started the process of purchasing his discharge from the RCMP. He had been with the force for a little more than eight years.

This young man must have been very aware of his inability to cope with things that appeared to involve more than routine danger but he had not taken any action to remove himself from the daily possibility of encountering such things. On the other hand, he had proven himself quite capable in most areas of police work and would have been a suitable candidate for an administrative post in some large centre. Having not taken steps to be transferred to such a post, he had been left with an ugly and difficult decision: face censure and punishment for failing to do his duty or leave the force. I believe he made the right choice for both himself and the RCMP.

Quesnel's Missing Man

Dave and I were working the graveyard shift on a chilly fall night when an excited motorist called to say that he had just seen a pickup truck take flight. The witness described the pickup passing him at tremendous speed and how, just as it started to pull back into the right lane, it went into a skid and spun completely around before leaving the road on the right-hand side and striking an intersecting roadway. The vehicle then became airborne, flying end over end until it landed in the highway ditch well beyond the road grade that it had hit. Our witness told us that there had been two men in the truck and they had been thrown out as the truck flew over the side road. They were both alive but obviously badly injured as they were screaming in pain and cursing loudly.

We called for an ambulance and a tow truck and set out in full emergency mode to drive the three-plus kilometres to the scene. Since the road surface was dry and there was good nighttime visibility throughout the area, as we drove along we speculated that the cause of this incident would no doubt be a drinking binge. At the scene we found that our witness had returned after using a pay phone to call us and was doing whatever he could to comfort the two men lying in the ditch near the wrecked pickup truck and reassure them that an ambulance was on the way. The fact that they were still alive was a miracle in itself.

The ambulance arrived only a moment behind us and we assisted in loading the two victims onto stretchers. They were hurting but conscious and quite abusive to us when we attempted to identify the driver but the smell of their breath, their actions and conduct left no doubt that they were drunk. Years of experience told us that if they had not been extremely drunk, they would never have survived such an incident. One appeared to have broken ribs and the other a compound fracture of his left forearm. Both had severe gravel rash from coming into intimate contact with the bottom of the highway ditch while still carrying a lot of forward momentum from the vehicle and falling from perhaps three metres or more above the ground.

As soon as the two assholes had been loaded into the ambulance and removed from the scene, the emergency was over. We could then work at our leisure to record the scene with photographs and take measurements before having the totally wrecked vehicle removed. Of course, in the specialized police world of today there are investigative resources available to reconstruct such an incident in every intimate detail. The police would pinpoint the exact spot where the vehicle first went out of control, the probable speed at various critical points along the trajectory and which part of the unit first came into contact with the intersecting road grade. Scientific examination of the flight path of the truck after it hit the intersecting road would even give them a very close approximation of how high the truck was above the ground when the two men parted company with it. As we were still quite a few years away from the introduction of the accident analysis program, any accident reconstruction efforts at this scene were left to Dave and myself with the help of the man who had witnessed the crash. It would be entirely up to us to gather the evidence to support charges of impaired driving or possibly criminal negligence causing death.

We took measurements along the flat, straight roadway and did our best to figure out the course of events from the time the pickup passed our witness's car to the final location of the wreckage. We concluded that the truck must have been at least three metres in the air at the moment the bodies were thrown out. This and the forward speed of the flying wreckage left us to conclude that the Grim Reaper must have been extremely busy somewhere else at that moment. The skid and yaw marks on the highway indicated that the vehicle had been over-steered to the extent that it went into a spin. There were no indications of braking over the entire length of the marks. At about their mid-point on the highway was a pool of beer mixed with crushed glass and cardboard showing that a full or nearly full case of beer had burst as it contacted the asphalt surface. We were not able to positively determine if the beer had been in the open box of the truck or if it was with the men in the cab but our educated guess was that the liquor would have been within easy reach of the cab's occupants just in case they were seized by a sudden thirst.

The preliminaries at the scene were completed in about an hour and a half and the tow truck collected the remains of what had been a fairly new vehicle, one that would never be on the road again. It was now approaching three in the morning so Dave and I attended our favourite all-night coffee spot for a shot of stay-awake and then attended at the hospital to make another attempt to get straight answers from the survivors. We found them somewhat mellowed by anaesthetic mixed with liquor and pain. The first of the two immediately asked us about Leroy's whereabouts.

"He's right across the hall," I told him.

"No! That's Pete!"

A very noticeable tightness seized our abdomens. Dave immediately went across the hall to interview the man in the other bed and confirmed our fears: there had been three persons in the truck—Leroy, Pete and Bubba.

Fear and panic reigned supreme!

We left the hospital and sped back to the accident location. Darkness was still fully with us as we began to search the area. The most likely location for the missing man seemed to be near where the other two had been dumped out as the vehicle flew over the intersecting roadway. When we found nothing there, we began to search back toward the point where the truck had first gone out of control, and that's where we found the missing man. He was lying curled up in a fetal position in the opposite ditch, adjacent to where the case of beer had burst on the highway. He was shivering violently but although he had a severe gravel rash, he had no obviously broken bones. As none of the three were wearing seatbelts, which was entirely normal conduct in those years, we figured he must have been dumped out of the cab during the first part of the end-for-end rotational skid. We speculated that in his drunken stupor, he may have neglected to close the door at the outset of their trip or he may have been distracted in a desperate attempt to save their last case of beer.

We could see that he had first touched down in thick bulrushes and soft earth before coming to rest on the dry gravel at the outside edge of the ditch. The path cut through the bulrushes by his flying body was clearly visible once we knew he was out there someplace but we'd had no reason to look there at the beginning of the investigation because we believed there were only two men. The man in the bulrushes may have been unconscious during the hour and a half we were on the scene the first time or he may have chosen to remain undetected. A belly full of liquor can result in some very strange actions by the owner thereof.

Once again we called the ambulance, the man was taken to the hospital and the on-call doctor was again rousted out of his bed to look after this straggler. All three were released from hospital by noon the following day. No charges were ever laid because we could not conclusively put any of the three behind the wheel but there was every indication that the missing man had been the driver. How or why he had abandoned the vehicle at such an early opportunity was never established. He obviously made the prudent decision—if one is inclined to give him credit for such clear thinking at that moment.

The Lead-Lined Camera Case

Our detachment first became aware that a full-time identification man was to be stationed with us when we were asked to find an office where he could set up his equipment. As this would normally include a photographic dark room, we were provided with exact specifications and in a short time we located a suitable site. The new man would not be arriving for several months but as the office was judged to be ideal for his needs and very well located in relation to our main office the rental agreement was signed in advance.

Within a few weeks of the office being secured, equipment for the new section began to arrive at the detachment. The smaller pieces were stored at our main office and larger things were immediately taken to the newly rented office. One of the nicest pieces of the new equipment was a very well-made camera case. Its outer shell was thin, strong, embossed aluminum with fancy gusseted and riveted outer corner reinforcements. The

The Lead-Lined Camera Case

interior of the case was deeply waffled foam rubber with custom-formed recesses to hold the camera and flash unit and a few other common articles used in photography work. Several of us were involved in hobby photography but we were definitely not able to afford such a deluxe piece of equipment so there may have been a few green eyes around the building. As none of us had met the new identification man up to that time, however, there was no justifiable reason for what happened over the next few days. It will just have to be catalogued under stupid and mean stunts.

A short time later one of the guys happened to make a routine call to the scrap metal dealer's yard in connection with an investigation he was working on and while there he saw a large quantity of lead sheeting approximately three millimetres thick and in slabs of various sizes. He immediately bought two pieces of this heavy material, each about fifty centimetres square, and carted them back to the office. The fancy new camera case was brought from the storage room. We had already learned that its foam rubber lining was only held into the case by the close fit, which required a slight compression of the material, so it was easily removed. This knowledge made the possibilities endless.

We removed the lining and made careful measurements before cutting the two lead slabs so they would be a very close fit against the top and bottom of the aluminum case. The malleable lead was then pressed into the empty case until it fit as if the manufacturer had intended it to be there. When we replaced the foam rubber, it was a perfect fit and the only evidence of our handiwork was the heft of the altered case; it was now over four kilograms heavier than it was intended to be.

In due course the new man arrived and set up his identification facilities. Over the next three years he was frequently called out to accidents and other events and he did some very effective work on behalf of us all. In addition, he was a cheerful and good-spirited fellow and we all enjoyed working with him. When he was advised at the end of his third year with us that he was to be transferred to another location, only one-half of the original conspirators were still working there but we all turned out for the farewell party, both out of respect for our departing workmate and to witness the unveiling of our secret dirty work. The camera case was brought in with great fanfare and the secret additions were pointed out to the victim. There were a lot of laughs about this prank and the victim told several stories about having to carry the camera case and equipment into some very remote locations, and he always wondered why the damned thing was so heavy.

Big Coal Mines and Big Money

In the summer of 1982 I transferred to Prince George to take charge of the city traffic and provincial highway patrol units, both of which operated out of the main police building in the downtown area. I had arrived right in the middle of the years that the Northeast Coal Project was under development in Tumbler Ridge to satisfy a contract with Japan to provide 100 million tonnes of metallurgical coal over a fifteen-year period. Along with the construction of all the facilities necessary for operating the massive Quintette and Bullmoose open pits mines, an entirely new town had to be built, along with 130 kilometres of railway lines, nearly sixteen kilometres of tunnels through the mountains, two highways and a power line all the way to Hudson's Hope. Like all mega-projects, this one attracted workers from all over Canada, not only due to the large number needed but also because of the potential for big paycheques. On projects of this kind the hourly rates for machine operators and truck drivers were about 50 percent over what these same people could make at similar jobs in most other parts of the country.

Although the city of Prince George lies some four hundred kilometres by road south and west of the project, some of the city's businesses did benefit through supplying parts and materials. But as police officers, we were seeing a different kind of effect: changes in the city's traffic patterns a few hours after the shifts changed at Tumbler Ridge. As there were strict deadlines for completion of the project and shipping the first coal to Japan, the work schedules at the many construction sites were set up so the men could put in very long shifts over a concentrated period of time and then have a substantial number of days off. At that time there were very limited recreational facilities in the partially completed new town and most of the workers had families and/or girlfriends in the more southerly areas of the province so on their days off many of them would drive all the way to the Vancouver area to blow off some accumulated "camp stink." They didn't want to spend a minute longer on the road than was absolutely necessary, and they knew that once they got to Prince George, there remained only a little more than eight hundred kilometres between them and the lights of Vancouver. These facts combined to cause some very extreme driving behaviour and the traffic patrolmen from my office had many stories about the drivers from the Northeast Coal Project and their reckless disregard for speed laws and road safety in general.

Both law enforcement and our court systems are well known for their glacier-like movement when adapting to new circumstances and in the early 1980s traffic fines were still fixed at the same amounts they had been at for decades: twenty-five dollars was the penalty for a speeding violation regardless of the offender's speed. Our only option in really extreme situations was to go for a charge of dangerous driving under the Criminal Code and several such charges had already been laid against workers from the project. This had little or no effect on their driving habits, however, because they had pockets full of money, they had not seen their wives or girlfriends for some time and they were feeling invincible. Their biggest concern when stopped by the police was the time they were losing while the ticket was issued.

Around 10:00 p.m. one early fall night two of our traffic guys were called to a serious crash about sixteen kilometres north of Prince George. The caller said only that a car had hit a moose. At the crash scene the guys found a passenger car with very extensive damage to its front end and its entire upper portion. The driver and the front seat passenger had died instantly, as had the moose. Bits and pieces of the car and the moose were scattered over a half-kilometre-long stretch of the road. The car, which had remained on its wheels throughout, and the debris field had only left the paved surface and entered a shallow ditch at the very end of their trip. The officers learned that the lone survivor had been sitting in the back seat of the car but he had come into very intimate contact

The Peace River Dam, located near Hudson's Hope, was the first of northeast BC's mega projects and provided thousands of jobs during its construction.

with the moose—or at least parts of it. He had that moose and its contents in his eyes, ears, nose and throat, but having escaped serious injury, he will, I suspect, always remember the night that he and most of a moose went for a short ride.

When our guys arrived, there were several vehicles stopped at the scene and two of the drivers reported that the demolished vehicle or one very similar to it had passed them just a few kilometres before the crash site as if they had been backing up. Another Tumbler Ridge construction worker told the police that there was obviously no need to think about or provide any first aid or assistance for the two men in the front seat of the car. He had actually seen the crash and had assisted the survivor out of the wreckage. This man had been driving a very high-powered pickup truck and, like the three in the car, had been on his way to the Vancouver area. He said that just prior to the accident he had been driving at about ninety when the car had passed him. It had been well clear of him and had started to return to the right lane when he saw its brake lights flash and at almost the same instant there was complete darkness ahead. He heard and felt an explosive impact as a shock wave bumped his vehicle. Knowing something had gone very wrong, he had braked hard, but before he was able to stop he was into the debris field. Fortunately he did not strike anything that caused further damage or injury. In confirming this witness's statement the police officer repeated his words about travelling at ninety kilometres per hour but the witness cut in to clarify that he was driving at ninety miles per hour just prior to the pass.

No charges were pursued against any of the people involved. The mess was cleared from the roadway and the incident was given as much publicity as we could arrange, particularly around the construction site.

The Fighting Fools

The main characters in this story were three brothers who had been born and raised in a rough and tumble home in the beautiful northern city of Prince George. They were about as close in age as the human reproductive system will allow and nearly identical in build and temperament. Their father and uncles and a variety of other tough northern men had taught them to settle any and all differences with their fists. As their pugilistic father advised them, "Never take no shit from nobody." The three had learned their lessons well, but fortunately for us at the police establishment and the many civilians who found themselves in conflict with these young men, they were only about average height and weight.

As soon as the youngest of the three reached the legal drinking age of nineteen they spent most of their evenings and weekends in the drinking establishments of the old downtown area of Prince George, which police officers referred to as the "gonorrhea racetrack." We were all cautioned not to attend calls to this area alone if it could be avoided but at that time we were still duty bound to get police aid to people who requested it and to do so without delay. With these conflicting factors in place we often found ourselves alone on the "racetrack."

By this time the three brothers had become part of the colourful subculture of that part of their city. They would never back away from a fight and had acquired a reputation for their frequent battles but they were also very skilled at goading other patrons of the "racetrack" into fights. We did observe, however, that nearly all of their losing sparring partners were quite drunk. We were never totally sure if this was because the locals would have to be quite drunk to take them on or if the brothers only chose opponents who were exhibiting the slowing and dulling effects of excessive alcohol consumption. In either case, these boys were soon well known in all the watering holes of Prince George and for a considerable distance along each road leading to or from it. Interestingly, while they loved to fight, they abstained from most other anti-social behaviour and most of the time they all held down jobs at the mills or in shops in the city. Their drug of choice was alcohol and they would have little or nothing to do with any of the street drugs that were becoming commonplace during that era.

At that time I was very fortunate to be the supervisor of an excellent group of dedicated traffic officers who all liked to get on with the tasks at hand but we had to endure all the (cop on cop) trash talk from the other police units in our building in spite of the fact that traffic people were the most frequent providers of backup for them all. One of the most frequently used degrading comments that was directed toward us was "I'd sooner have a sister in a whorehouse than a brother on traffic." We on the traffic unit got in our shots whenever the opportunity arose but we did not have any patented lines like that one.

One of the most outstanding members of my unit at that time was a young corporal whom I will call Grant, a fine young man who took great pride in his physical fitness and strength. He would frequently jog sixteen kilometres after doing a workout on the weight bench; anything under sixteen kilometres and he would hardly break a sweat. Grant rode the police motorcycle and loved it and whenever he was out on that motorcycle something was about to happen. He dealt with a great number of traffic violations and frequently found occupied stolen vehicles, vehicles with drugs on board and an amazing variety of other criminal activities. He dealt with each incident quickly and efficiently in order to get back to the roadwork that he so enjoyed. In a very short time he had established a reputation as someone who could handle himself in any of the situations he encountered while doing his duty. He was not as notorious around Prince George as the three brothers but perhaps he should have been.

One beautiful Saturday afternoon in spring Grant was out on the motorcycle near the northern boundary of the city when he heard frequent radio calls for a general duty car to attend to a disturbance complaint at a nearby business. As there seemed to be no one available or willing to attend the call from the general police members, Grant radioed that he would go. He advised the dispatch centre that he was on the motorcycle so he would need a car to attend as well in case an arrest was necessary.

The call had come from the staff at the local Dairy Queen where three drunken men were causing a disturbance. Grant rode into the parking lot, put the police motorcycle on its stand and headed for the place of business. As soon as he'd heard the details of the call he had thought of the notorious brothers whom he knew from numerous encounters around the "gonorrhea racetrack" and his suspicions were confirmed even before he opened the glass door of the restaurant. Once inside, he walked directly over to the table where the three brothers were sitting. Having decided that he would embarrass them into leaving the restaurant if he could he began the conversation by calling each of them by name and telling them that their behaviour was frightening the kids and their mothers who were in the restaurant and that they should do the right thing and leave immediately. The brothers had a load of alcohol in their systems but Grant's direct approach caught them a little off their game. They lurched to their feet and began to apologize to Grant and to the people in the restaurant. Detecting the momentum in his favour, Grant pushed verbally for them to be on their way and they were out the door within two minutes of his arrival.

Grant then spoke briefly to the restaurant manager before going out to keep an eye on the "Three Stooges." Although they lived nearby, he doubted very much that they had walked to the Dairy Queen and he suspected that they might get into a vehicle in their drunken condition.

The three were feeling a little down on themselves, however, for being shamed out of the restaurant by a single cop, and as they walked by the parked police motorcycle, one of them decided to tip it over to demonstrate their unhappiness.

They should not have done that!

Just as the motorcycle fell on its side Grant came out of the restaurant on the run. Their disrespect had aroused his competitive spirit. In the ensuing battle the brothers gave it their very best as they had a reputation to maintain and the three of them certainly proved their toughness that afternoon because their combined efforts just about took Grant. In this instance. however, their opponent was cold sober and the last of the trio went down just as the backup car arrived, and very wisely he chose not to get up again. Later Grant told me that he was about done by the time he got the last one. In spite of that he walked over to the overturned motorcycle and put it upright with a single movement that required both strength and coordination. Then he got onto the cycle and rode away—though only until he was out of sight of the crowd that had gathered around the fight. He then took time out to gather himself.

The legend of the lone policeman who took the big three spread around the city like a wildfire. There is much to be said for and about street justice but a happening like that one went a long way toward making a tough job a lot easier for the rest of us.

It was about mid-summer of that same year when Jim, another of my men, was patrolling the city on the motorcycle. Once again frequent calls came over the radio for a car to attend a disturbance at one of the bars on the "racetrack" but none of the general duty members answered. Obviously they were all very busy. Jim responded from the motorcycle to say he was nearby and would attend but a car would still be required if an arrest had to be made. He parked the motorcycle at a garage business just around the corner from the source of the calls. The people who owned and worked at this business were well known to us and could be counted on to keep vandals away from our equipment.

Jim walked around the corner of the hotel to find most of the crowd from the beer parlour had spilled out onto the street to watch a fight. As the fight was about over, his arrival got the full attention of the half-drunken crowd and when a couple of loud-mouths got the crowd excited Jim quickly found himself surrounded by a mob that seemed intent on beating the crap out of him. He had his back to the wall of the hotel, trying to identify as many of the mob as he could and all the while fully expecting to get a beating or worse. During this brief time he became aware of someone from the crowd moving toward him along the hotel wall. He thought this would be the beginning of the battle, but as he turned to identify this person, he recognized one of the three legendary brothers. The fellow gave him a big smile.

"Looks like you could use a hand," he said.

As soon as this fellow offered assistance, the crowd dispersed. No doubt this sudden change in events was due in a large part to the reputation of Jim's helper. Jim thanked him heartily but his new friend said that the only reason he had done it was to be where the action was best. He was truly disappointed that the crowd had broken up before there were at least a few fisticuffs.

Jim was definitely the racetrack winner that day.